MW01518054

FISHING

the

QUEEN CHARLOTTE ISLANDS

by

BOB LONG

Published by
Raser Enterprises Ltd.
1988.

Canadian Cataloguing in Publication Data

Long, Bob, 1951-
     Fishing the Queen Charlotte Islands

ISBN 0-9693727-0-1

     1.Fishing - British Cloumbia - Queen Charlotte Islands - Guide-books. I. Title.
SH572.B7L65 1988 799.1' 09711' 31 C88-091639-7

Illustrations by Maureen Benoit

Published by Raser Enterprises Ltd.
     Box 459, Sandspit, B.C. V0T 1T0 or C-412,
     108 Mile Ranch, 100 Mile House, B.C. V0K 2E0
     604-791-6256
Printed in Canada

     This book was completely produced on the Queen Charlotte Islands, except printing.

To my wife Sherry who
has put up with all this
fishing!

Contents

Contents continues

Preface:

When I was a boy I used to hear stories about fishing trips, I can't remember specifics but I do remember my grandfather and his fishing gear. These are the cane rods, so rare now, reverently cared for by Grampa, carefully returned to their rack after each trip, smelling of silk line grease and wet wool. I have great memories of the same aroma from Grampa's Dodge sedan on our way back from Lakelse Lake, with me too small to see over the dash.

These are the same cane rods I later 'stole' from my Dad, rods which now occupy the same revered place in my study. My dad says they were just cheap hardware specials, only worth a few dollars, but to me they are priceless, a reminder of my grandfather.

Memories are important. My passion for sports fishing starts with memories of my Grandfather. Of course my Dad was the one that first took me to Millionaires Pool on the Babine River where the wasps stung me too many times. The first fly-in trip to one of the lakes around Prince Rupert in an old Cee Bee pusher aircraft. We found Canada goose eggs in a nest on an island, and the devils club was as tall as regular spruce trees. I don't know the name of the lake but its memory is forever etched in my mind.

I remember days spent fishing for fingerling coho in the tiny streams that feed Lakelse Lake, with tiny hooks and little rolled up balls of white bread.

We all have these starts to a life long ambition of a plus 50 pound spring salmon, a 25 pound steelhead, a 20 pound coho and a plus 200 pound halibut.

I progressed to taking my friends fishing, and spending my hard earned money on float plane trips to Muddy Lake or Ian Lake or a hundred other lakes. Bought boats, big and small, to get to the fishing. Spent money on maps and charts of the whole B.C. coast and pored over them night after night searching for new unknown fishing places.

Soon my wife was the target of my fishing ways, she would go with me on our holidays to the Queen Charlotte Islands (she didn't mind too much since her parents have lived there most of their lives) and have our Boston Whaler skiff float away with the big tides in July, only to be found a 100 yards down the beach in the morning. Tough going ? Yes, especially when the tide comes into the tent in the middle of the night, (But dear, I thought we were high enough up the beach!)

We lived in Campbell River where--I have to stress--I had no choice but to join right in, and spend hours attempting to catch a few Spring salmon. Then to Port Hardy where I fine tuned my love for light tackle coho fishing. Sherry, my wife, was pregnant and I made one too few pit stops and was minus my long term fishing partner. Sherry took up child raising and I kept fishing.

Finally the day came. Sherry decided to help me get this fishing out of my system once and for all time. We moved to the Charlottes. She gave me one year off to spend my youth.

Well, that was seven years ago and going strong. Thanks Sherry I couldn't have done it without you!

The Charlottes brought an uncharted opportunity to fish, and fish I did. Coho, Spring and Halibut, Trout, Steelhead and more, there is no end to the available challenge.

During my days commercial fishing I had been to the Charlottes to fall fish for Coho in South Moresby. The fishing had
been good and I always wanted to come back. As soon as I
arrived on the Charlottes I immediately headed south to the
places I remembered. The fishing was better than great, and I
decided to develop a floating sports fishing camp. That is, a
cabin on a raft of logs all lashed together. It worked and for four
years I and many friends, clients and family had a wonderful
time fishing the Juan Perez Sound open ocean coho salmon.

With the coming of this so-called National Park it was
obvious to those of us living on the Charlottes that what we had
built up would soon be gone. Parks Canada wanted a $70,000
sewage disposal plant on a $10,000 cabin and float!

The fish are still there, they don't understand politics,-they
live there. In a few years the beauty of the place will be
destroyed by the bureaucrats and the Haidas in a big hurry to
cash in on the people rush. Gone forever is the quiet bath at
Hotspring Island and the friendly hand from the guys at Frank
Beban's Lyell Island logging camp. Gone are the John Mac
Laughlins who had logged in South Moresby since he was a
kid, as his dad before him. A sad commentary on the live-and-
let-live concept this country runs on. The Toronto idiots have
had their way.

But back to fishing. There is no place like the Queen Charlotte Islands. The Islands are their own mini-continent with all
the different fishing landscapes to choose from. I have tried to
put these landscapes down in a systematic way, so that you can
take a short cut to effective fishing. Some locals may resent this
information being made public, but there is enough room and
enough new areas to discover, that I don't think that feeling will
last.

Like all fishermen, I know you enjoy stories about fishing
and the people involved, so I have included some Charlotte
fishing stories for your enjoyment. Hard lines!

Section : Salmon

Story : Frank Beban's Last Smiley

Frank Beban loved to fish for Spring salmon, or as he called them "smileys". That term for Spring salmon comes from the commercial trolling fleet and was explained by Frank as "when you catch one you just can't stop smiling."

Frank Beban was born and raised in Nanaimo. Frank was a logger, and a good one. He built Frank Beban Logging Ltd. from one piece of equipment on the central coast into a multi-million dollar logging concern. Frank was a logger's logger, a risk taker and a true west coast legend.

When I first met Frank he was anchored at Henslung Cove, Langara Island, fishing and beach combing with his wife Dolores, and two of his young daughters. He was on the Reef Island, a 41-foot fibre glass combination tow boat and pleasure craft. This craft was well-appointed and Frank was proud of her. I was the deckhand on the Northern Breeze skippered by Ralph Deinstadt, packing salmon to Prince Rupert from Langara Island. Once Ralph and Frank met, they realized they had something in common, the love of a drink, (nay - a bottle!) of Crown Royal.

Frank, Ralph and I stayed up too late that night talking fishing and other issues, mixing fishing and politics. That was the summer of 1972 and it is hard to imagine writing this 16 years later using the same setting. So much has changed already.

Frank died of a heart attack on Lyell Island July 26, 1987 but not before he caught a 52 pound smiley off Coho Point, Langara Island two weeks earlier. Frank was always a large man, probably near 300 pounds when he died. He was huge both in actions and in heart. If he liked you, you need only ask for his shirt to be wearing it.

Frank loved to fish for Springs as his father before. The Bebans have always had sports fishing camps on the B.C. coast. The first to fish Hakai Pass, a cabin at Stuart Island, you name it, Frank or his dad had fished it. The Beban Logging company always had a Beaver aircraft to fish or hunt with and in the years on the Charlottes, helicopters to increase the access to streams and lakes for trout and steelhead fishing. There are hundreds of lucky sports fishermen that have enjoyed the legendary Beban hospitality.

Langara Island is the latest hot spot for fishing Spring Salmon on the coast. Frank discovered Langara's fishing through his ownership of a commercial salmon troller, and personal exploration in the early 1970's.

I spoke with Frank about a small float camp he wanted to build for Langara Island fishing. He had the design in his head, like you remember your social insurance number. The cabin would be 36 feet by whatever, kitchen here, as he sketched it out on the back of a coaster. "We found that that was the best design from the one we built for Hakai Pass," he said.

The summer of 1987 was a good year for sports fishing at Langara with many large Springs caught. Frank had his new Reef Island, a 53 ft. Canoe Cove beauty complete with everything imagineable, sonar, radar, loran, shower, anchored in Henslung Cove. He was there to catch fish, big ones if possible. The commercial trolling season was to open on the first of July, so Frank scheduled some time in the middle of June. Mooching from a small 14-foot boat with cut-plug herring was Frank's favourite. Light tackle with special drop weights on a good mooching rod were the effective tools of this man's arsenal.

Fishing Coho point and other spots at Langara was the normal activity for a Frank Beban fishing party. This particular day Jim Connor, manager for MacMillian-Bloedel, arrived with some guests on his 26 foot fibreglass cruiser. Frank immediately invited them to tie up and come aboard for some good cheer. For the next three days Jim Connor and party were honoured with the true Beban hospitality.

Frank was after the big one and knew that the flood tide at Coho point was a good bet. Frank's brother-in-law went out this particular afternoon as helmsman. As usual Frank was the captain. Everyone else was mooching with cut-plug herring until we heard the commotion of Captain Frank with a fish on. Three hundred pounds of loud and jubilant man in a 14-foot boat, and a very large 'Smiley' on the end of light line gives you a sportsman's symphony. The battle splashed in circle after circle as Frank and the fish tired. By using the boats maneuverability, the helmsman was able to maintain the position Frank needed to tire this big silver and purple fighter.

Forty-five minutes later it was time to celebrate. Tugging the scales at 52 pounds, this was the fish Captain Beban was fishing for. He caught this beauty with his tackle on his point on a day that Poiseden had sent to complete a true sportsman's accomplishments. The reward of a flat calm evening, no wind, good friends and a tremendous Smiley.

That night Frank Beban poached his prize and garnished it with butter, lemon juice and oregano. Coupled with a fresh green salad and excellent red and white French wine the meal could not be matched in any restaurant in the world. Country and Western music playing in the background and some ubiquitous Crown Royal finished off a truly exceptional day. Poker and fishing stories lasted until the early morning with Frank right in there. Next morning brought Frank up to make coffee and breakfast, with a few of the younger fishers still in their bunks.

Over the years that Frank Beban, his company, and his employees were harassed by the environmentalists and the Haida Indians, Frank tried to be fair to all involved. He always

16

gave donations to any worthy cause, helped the communities of the Charlottes with all manner of access to his organizations with free this and free that. He gave the Haida Indians many cedars to carve from his Lyell Island operation. This was a Prince of a man. I am sad that he was not treated better by all who were involved with the South Moresby debate.

Many will remember Frank as the big guy on T.V. on Lyell Island representing the law of the land with the words, "Please step aside you are breaking the law".

Spring Salmon

Life Cycle • Catch Methods • Feeding Habits
Timing & Location • Fishing Areas
Story : Clint Cameron Visits

Life Cycle:

The life cycle of the Spring Salmon is wonderful in its simplicity. A pair of fish spawn and die and the offspring eventually return to that same stream, to again complete the cycle of spawning and dying. On the Queen Charlotte Islands there is only one river that hosts the large Spring Salmon, the Yakoun. The Yakoun River Spring run has been protected from fishing for years because of its small numbers of fish. No other stream or river has spawning Springs, although there is a suggestion that Government will soon plant Springs in a West coast stream. Spring Salmon that have smolted and are feeding in the ocean know the Queen Charlotte Islands are perfect for foraging and feeding and they are present almost all year around in some numbers.

Fishing for these Springs involves the hunting of these feeding fish that are eventually headed to some larger river system to spawn. The Skeena, Fraser, Columbia and more are the natal streams for many of our Charlotte Spring Salmon.

Catch methods:

For the first few years I fished in the Charlottes I used the standard mooch and troll methods that worked so well in Campbell River and Port Hardy. Because there is little fishable moving water in the Charlottes the best catch method is to troll slowly with cut-plug or whole firecracker size bait. In those days, frozen herring was hard to come by, and what was available was to the commercial fleet as halibut bait; ten pounds of herring frozen in one big lump. I would buy a years worth of sports herring from Vancouver and have it flown up on what was then Pacific Western Airline's 737 jet.

Today, frozen bait is in many stores on the Charlottes, especially the sporting goods stores, Mavis's in Sandspit and Meegan's in Charlotte.

Some fishermen here use strip herring with a teaser of some sort, this is usually terminal to a number one 'Ab & Al' flasher. This gear works well: if you like it use it.

I think flasher gear is really a hangover from the commercial fishing days of past decades. I have never had the need to use a flasher or dodger in the Charlottes to find success. I've had very few days when the flasher gang has out fished me. Flasher gear reduces the fish's ability to show their stuff, causes more gear drag, costs more to lose and most importantly, encourages the rod into a rod holder.

It is my contention that more fish are lost because the rod is not in your hand, than any other reason. A tremendous amount of FUN is lost also. Without high line drag caused by flashers, dodgers, planning devices, the fisherman can hold the rod in his/her hand. The fish strikes and you hit it! It's natural; if you missed the fish you were part of the best event anyway. Forget the rod holder, you want it to be: just you and the fish.

I hope I have convinced you about holding the rod,(an extension of your arm,) in your hand at all times. Sure it's hard to drink beer at the same time, but you're out there to fish - drink beer with the pretty girls in the Sandspit Inn. I regularly fish by myself with two fly rods, one in each hand and steer my Boston Whaler (tiller handle) all at the same time, it takes some practice but it can be done. I even have the odd beer too.

Classic mooching is really trolling a herring but letting the moving water give the bait some action. As I mentioned before there is very little moving water on the Charlottes that is fishy, so I simply move the boat slowly to give the bait its action. Mooch trolling I call it. This is the same method used in Rivers Inlet, and other locations where there is no moving water.

Weight is our next issue I never use more than 4 ounces in the banana weight variety (swivels on both ends), these weights are also useful for Coho fishing. I use 4 ounce, 3 ounce, 2 ounce and in some cases 1 ounce weights. There are times that you will go heavier, say at Langara to get down faster and fish deeper. This fishing is done with the regular mooching/trolling rods 8 to 10 feet. I like my old '1264 Fenwick' from Campbell River, but any good moocher will do. The rod should have some action in the end to sense a fish's take. Remember this is much easier because you are holding your rod, right!

Tensile strength of you monofiliment mainline should be 20 to 25 pound test with 15, 18, or 20 pound leaders. The lighter strength leader will increase your hooking rate but also increase your break-offs. It is your choice.

If down riggers are your cup of tea, then I can't help much. I don't use them because there is no need to. If you wish , go ahead. Use them as you would anywhere else, they work well but, they are not as much FUN.

We have talked about fishing with bait. What about other terminal gear? I use four other types for both Springs and Cohoes, small plugs, bucktail flies with or without small spinners, hoochies and flashtail flies. This same terminal gear can be used with flashers also. The standard is the green and white hoochie or flashtail behind a flasher / dodger.

Jigging with stingzildas or buzzbombs is not a well-used method on the Charlottes, but under the right conditions they can be deadly on Spring salmon.

I use herring , flies and 2 1/2 inch plugs for Spring salmon fishing. The herring is by far the most productive, but I have caught June Springs on the Sandspit bar with these small plugs and flies.

Feeding habits:

Some general comments on how to catch Spring salmon using knowledge of their feeding habits. Spring salmon don't seem to like the surface of the ocean, they don't feed at the top of the water column (unlike Coho). Sure, sometimes they are seen on the surface after bait, but as a rule they are caught farther down in the water column. My observation is that Springs are caught by fishing under their prey, many times this is very near the bottom, but other times it is just under the school of herring or needle fish they are feeding on. Placing your bait on the edge and just under the feed is the most effective method. These observations are made mostly from mooch trolling with cut-plug herring but I think they are universal in their application.

Now for some specifics: Springs feed on spawning herring early in the year (April or May), when the herring are spawning on the Charlottes' kelp. These fish are strong, open ocean fish usually in the 20 to 30 pound class. To catch these fish you need to fish before the herring spawn because the milt in the water from the male herring seems to repel herring predators. So timing is important. Check with the locals about the year-to-year timing of the spawn. Just call the local sporting goods store for that information.

Timing & Location :

With the weather being bad at this time of year not a lot of fishing takes place, so information on location is scarce. We know that there are Springs in Skidegate Inlet during this spawning period, and some fish at Sewell Point (see chart) but much remains unknown. There are herring spawns at Port Louis on the West Coast of the Charlottes, Juan Perez Sound in South Moresby, Skincuttle Inlet in South Moresby, Louscoone Inlet in South Moresby and other locations. No one knows about the fishing in these areas, but the commercial herring seine fleet does catch spring salmon in its nets when fishing for bait herring, so we know that they are there. Logic says that good Spring salmon fishing should be available wherever a concentration of prey exists. I will leave this challenge to the hardy souls that love the vulgar weather the Charlottes experiences at this time of year.

Added benefits to fishing at this time of the year include the regular sighting of the migrating Gray Whales on the east coast of the Charlottes. They are feasting on the herring spawn deposited on the shallow eel grass flats. These great beasts can be regularly seen from the road in front of Sandspit and Skidegate during April and May.

Spring salmon feed on the needle fish that are ever present in the waters surrounding the Charlottes. I tie sparse bucktails and tube flies to imitate this prey. I think flashtail flies also imitate the needle fish. Springs and Coho target this prey at the beginning of the summer (May,June) particularly at the Sandspit spit (see chart). That is when my small plugs and flies work the best.

The last significant feed for Springs is the squid. Many post mortems have revealed the Spring salmon's love for this prey species. The July Spring salmon fishery in Cumshewa Inlet is probably triggered by the many squid there at that time. Although I have always caught fish with cut-plug herring I think a hoochie or other squid imitation might work better. Give it a try!

Where and when? I have suggested some timing in the foregoing but I'll go over it again in general and then go to the specifics when we talk about the, "Where?"

Generally the Spring Salmon fishing is in two seasons. Firstly, the fishery in conjunction with the herring spawn takes place in the months of April and May. The second season is June, July, August and some of September. This is the major Spring salmon season and the timing of most of the commercial and sports pressure. Timing can be important especially with regard to the start of the commercial trolling season. The commercial fleet targets Spring salmon on the West coast of the Charlottes, Langara Island and Dixon Entrance usually at the beginning of July. Sports fishing before this fleet arrives can increase your chances considerably. The same is true once the commercial troll fisheries close, some time at the end of August. That makes for a great fishery on the west coast of Skidegate Narrows, as in 1987. Many 50 and 60 plus pound fish were caught at the beginning of September that year.

Fishing Areas :

I have divided the areas to fish into two categories. "One", the areas easily accessed by small boats that are trailerable, and "Two" the areas that require larger boats, expert understanding of the Charlotte weather patterns, and a true sense of adventure.Some of the information on the second areas comes to me second hand and must be taken as that.

There are only two places to fish the herring spawn Spring salmon: Skidegate Inlet (see areas outlined) and Sewell Point area (see area outlined): the others should be left to the very expert.

The areas that are easier to get to and relatively sheltered to fish in the summer season are: the Sandspit Bar (see outline), the Cumshewa Inlet area (see outline) and the Masset Inlet Can-Buoy areas (see outline) all of these areas can have bad weather but they also hold Coho and Halibut . The Sandpsit Bar is good in July, Cumshewa Inlet is good in June and July having been hot around the beginning of July with the big tides. Masset Can-Buoy area is good starting in June and is fishable through September.

Langara Island, Seven Mile, Rennell Sound, West Coast of Skidegate Inlet, Juan Perez Sound, Richardson Point are all areas that are difficult if not impossible to get to. I will outline on the charts where the Spring salmon can be found at each location. Many other locations probably have Spring salmon for sports fishermen, but these spots have yet to be discovered. In Campbell River and Haiki Pass sports fishing has gone on for many years, so there is much more information on timing and fish location. In the Queen Charlotte Islands the areas are relatively unfished. Therefore, there is much more to learn.

The big Chinook are caught at Langara Island, West Coast of Skidegate Narrows and off Masset Inlet. A few are caught during the herring spawn fisheries in April in Skidegate Inlet. I have witnessed some 50 pounders from Cumshewa Inlet on the July 1st weekend. The charts will give you the information for fishing these areas but I recommend that you go to the existing Lodges. Langara Lodge, Peregrine Lodge in Naden Harbour, and the Oak Bay Marina Group's Charlotte Princess all operate at Langara Island and other Queen Charlotte " big fish" spots.

Story : Clint Cameron Visits

Clint Cameron is considered, even by competing guides, as one of the best spring salmon fishing guides in Campbell River. Clint and family operate the Dolphins resort in Campbell River and are active in the fishing life of their community. Clint is in his early thirties.

A few years back Clint decided that he had better do some exploratory fishing on the Queen Charlottes. I lived in Campbell River for a few years so mutual friends suggested that Clint look me up, which he did. Mr. Cameron arrived with his 17-foot Boston Whaler trailered behind his Jimmy four wheel drive. He was equipped with everything, trout rods, mooching gear, bait, waders, video camera and more.

Clinton and brother Greg had a client along, Dr. Neil Chamberlain, a long-time fishing partner. I could not go fishing immediately because I had to work a few days that week, but I promised to go on the weekend.

Neil, Greg and Clint fished around the Charlottes. They went to Rennell Sound and caught a halibut (about 60 pounds) and lost another one (bigger). They fished for spring salmon, their real target ,but without success.

On the weekend I suggested that we fish Mosquito Lake for trout. We caught many trout and had a great time. Clint has a live bait tank in his boat so we put the captured trout in the tank and picked out the best for our beach lunch before releasing the rest.

All the time Clinton was on my case about being the hot-shot guide for the Charlottes." Why couldn't I put them on some spring salmon," he kept saying. It was getting harder and harder to take, so I finally said that I would show them the "spot" tomorrow. Everyone laughed. Of course, I had no idea where to fish, it being the end of July. The west coast would be good but the wind was westerly and it would be too rough.

The year before, a Sandspit fisherman was out after abalone in Cumshewa Inlet, on the big tides at the beginning of July. He threw overboard a fishing line out of habit, and caught a 51 pound spring. In desperation I thought we would try there even though we were three weeks late.

That night with a few beers, the invective was very high. They smelled that I was not as confident as usual, and were setting up tomorrow as my big guide test. Most Campbell River guides have that competitive spirit. On this night I wished they'd left it at home.

The next morning the weather was fine and I thought we should fish the west coast, but too late, they had me committed to Cumshewa and were going to rub it in. All the way there everyone needled me about this "hot spot". It took a good two hours to arrive at the fishing location and I had taken to praying to the "Great Fish God" for success.

Campbell River guides know their cut-plug herring and we were soon fishing effectively just east of Conglomerate Point. Twenty minutes later and the comments were still coming fast and furious, when Neil gets a take and misses, but insists it was a spring salmon. I thought he was just being kind to me so that Clint and his brother would let up. Begrudgingly Clint turned to go back over the same spot, this time Neil hooked the fish solid, and played a 29 pound spring to the boat. Although he wanted to release the fish, I asked that we keep it for a barbecue, thinking that this fish was just a fluke. When I cleaned the fish it had Neil's first cut-plug herring in its stomach, I was impressed with Neil's understanding of this fish's actions. At least the comments stopped, but I said nothing.

The next pass and we had another strike and I was handed the rod, only to over-react and break off the 20 pound spring salmon. Next I broke-off a spring that jumped around the boat trailing the 3 ounce red banana weight. Finally the others were allowed to play fish and we caught and released many more spring salmon in the 20 to 25 pound class. I finally managed to get one to the boat for release also.

It was time to get even, and that I did. They bought the beer that night and I still get mileage every time I see Clint. Don't tell him, but some times the "luck" part of fishing plays a very large part in your trip.

Coho Salmon:

Life Cycle • General Comments
Catch Methods • Timing & Location
• River Fishing

Life Cycle:

Coho are an incredible salmon species, since they don't need special circumstances to propagate. On the Charlottes as elsewhere on the B.C. coast, coho can spawn in any small water course and, more importantly, they are willing to go the farthest upstream to find spawning habitat. Coho must rear in streams that have water pools throughout the summer months.

As opposed to Chum salmon and Pink salmon, which go to sea as soon as they hatch from the gravel, the coho spends its first summer in its home stream, feeding on the available food sources.

The next spring Coho migrate downstream to salt water where they smolt. This is a process whereby the 4 or 5 inch fresh water fish adapts to its new salt water environment. I have watched for hours as these little guys, at the edge of the fresh and salt water in the estuaries, adapt to their new chrome sided finishes.

One only needs to contemplate the thousands of eggs it took to produce this one healthy smolt. He still has the perils of the open ocean ahead of him.

For the life cycle of the Coho to continue, man must pay attention to this creature's stream home. In the Charlottes many of these small streams are protected by the local loggers who are also the most ardent Coho fishermen.

By far the Coho's largest danger comes from the over-fishing by both sports and commercial fishermen alike. A number of small enhancement projects are underway on the Charlottes by volunteers, to enhance the Coho runs. There is also a hatchery on the Pallant Creek in North Moresby that produces Cohos.

As a general rule the Charlotte Coho are doing quite well, however this will not be true in the future if the pressure from fishermen is concentrated on a few runs.

General Comments:

The capture of Coho salmon is my first love. Nothing can equal the maniacal charge of an open ocean Coho at your surface trolling bucktail fly, just 6 feet astern of the boat. This is the predator at turbine speed, about to fulfill its' genetically coded instruction-KILL! The tenacity of this Porsche on water wheels, as he slashes again and again at your fly ,has no equal.

The adrenaline rush of the fisherman is produced by the high pitched whine of the flyreel, defying centrifugal force and the monofilament's tensile strength. When your think you are in control , standing in the boat palming your warm reel, the fish imitates a Poseidon missile and rockets 6 feet into the air, the line goes limp, you've lost him! No, he was running towards the boat, now you can feel him, too late he's jumping again, and again.

Now you know why this is called sport, you're not in control; he is! If this fish is strong and lucky he will throw the hook. If he is not, you can always release him, to complete his rounding of third base to find his way to home stream. Or, you can dispatch him as swiftly as he would the needle fish and complete his place in the higher chain of consumption. It is your choice, you are finally in control again!

This is almost as good as sex!

Catch methods:

There are many methods used to catch this aggressive fish. Any method used for Spring salmon also works well on Coho, but the Coho deserves better.

Coho should be caught on light tackle so that they can show their aerial acrobatics. Monofilament mainline of 12, 15 and 18 pound test with 10 pound leaders will serve you well.

I've fished for the last five years almost exclusively with a number of small, red, white, and green bucktails and tube flies, some with small abalone spinners in front or behind.

I fish these flies on or near the surface with 3/8 and 5/8 ounce keel weights and many times without any weight at all in the classic skip fly method so popular on Vancouver Island.

The aggressive June, July, and August Coho are attracted by your outboard propeller and exhaust bubbles. I think these imitate a school of needle fish. Whatever it represents the Queen Charlotte Island Coho want those bubbles.

On occasion I've witnessed 5 or 6 fish charge out of these bubbles obviously hunting as a pack. The action can be thrilling to say the least, double headers and even triples are not uncommon.

Here is an example of how tough these coho can be to catch. I was fishing in South Moresby by myself, attempting to catch a few fish for an Ecosummer kayak tour that happened to be camped on one of my fishing beaches. I was using the same two fly rod method that I've mentioned earlier, and hooked two fish at the same time. I played one fish to the boat without problem and was about to reel in the other, (which conveniently lay quietly off the stern of the boat), when I turned the outboard motor and it fell off the transom. I still had hold of the outboard handle but of course the motor revved up at the same time. Now the coho decided that it was time to make a run and leap a few times.

In one hand I had the half throttled outboard and the other a full throttle coho. I got the motor slowed but I couldn't pull it in the boat one handed even though I was trying. By this time the people on the beach were cheering me on as they now understood my predicament.

Finally, I put the rod in the bottom of the boat and used two hands to bring the 20 horse power outboard inboard. This was done quickly enough to grab the rod before it was pulled overboard and unbelievably, especially to the beach spectators, I landed the other coho for their dinner. Which was tougher ? Well, I hate to admit it, but landing the Evinrude was a severe test.

34

Timing & Location:

Starting in May immature coho can be caught on the shallow flats directly east of the Sandspit bar. This area has tremendous coho fishing through July with the fish growing larger all the time. June 15 or so is the traditional date for great coho fishing off the spit for fish that are in the 6 pound class.

Needle fish school up on the spit and are the main food supply for cohos that are putting on a pound a month over the summer.

Skidegate Inlet is home for many coho later in the season, August to October as the fish consider the spawning ritual. Fishing along the beach right in Queen Charlotte City and the north beach of Moresby Island will net many fish.

August to October are the times to fish for the big coho in front of the Tlell and Copper Rivers. The middle of September for the Tlell and October for the Copper River.

Open ocean coho can be caught anywhere along the east coast of the Charlottes during June, July and August. I have indicated on the charts some of the more likely areas. To fish for these coho keep your eyes open because they always show themselves by jumping. The commercial trollers catch huge numbers of coho on the Dogfish Banks all summer.

The mouth of Masset Inlet in the vicinity of the red can-buoy and west along the beach towards Naden Harbour has coho during these same summer months. There is always a chance of a big spring salmon too.

The west coast of the Charlottes accessed through Skidegate Inlet or Rennell Sound always has coho in good numbers in addition to spring salmon. Remember the weather can be rough at the best of times, be prepared for the worst and don't contemplate this area for fishing without a good sized boat. The points of land are good areas to explore for coho and spring salmon. I have indicated some areas on the charts for you to try, but they are not the final word. Fish are where you find them!

There are times when Coho are fussy, and you need some finesse to catch them. As soon as the Coho starts thinking about spawning sometime in September and October they become less aggressive and you need to entice them. This can usually be done with spinning gear, or if you have more patience a cast fly.

Anything that is shiny and spins or wobbles will work, sometimes the fish go for one type or the other, but as a rule the Meeps, Crocodile, or Sneak types all work well.

Moresby Camp and Gillatt Arm is a case in point: the coho headed for the Pallant Creek in August and September are schooled up in the Arm and can be difficult to catch. A good method is to cast a spinner to the fish that are showing on the surface, remember to cast in front of these cruising fish and you will have your limit in no time at all.

With the enhancement of the Pallant Creek coho by the Government hatchery, fishing for these salmonids, some in the 20 pound class, will be good for many years to come.

Sewell Point and surrounding waters hold excellent coho in mid-September. Fishing with a bucktail fly and a small trailing spinner can be great fun. Along Sewell Rocks and across the bay at Selwyn Point and beach north can also be good fishing.

Cumshewa Inlet, at the head and along the north shore of Louise Island, especially in front of Mathers Creek, is a good coho producer in September. Coho also school all along the area eastward from Skedans Island and Low Island. Again hunt these fish by sight, they will always jump to tell you where they are.

Coho are present throughout Juan Perez Sound in July and August and in Houston Stewart Channel at the same time. There is very little sports fishing pressure on these areas so expect excellent fishing if you can find the schools of coho. This is exploratory fishing at its very best.

The fly fisherman can cast from the shore to estuary fish or from a boat to catch open ocean coho. Fishing can be sight casting to each fish or blind casting to where the fish should be lying.

Pallant Creek Coho will take a cast fly at the mouth of the creek in September, but it will be hard to find a quiet moment without some spincasting or roe fishing friend disturbing the fish holding for the tide. The fish usually only strike a fly when the tide's salt water first hits the fish holding in the estuary's fresh water. This is the most exciting fly fishing for salmon anyone can experience. Although these Coho can not rival a fresh steelhead in the river the Coho is the steelhead's equal when in salt water.

All coho streams will present an opportunity to do some fly casting to fish waiting to run up-stream and spawn. Some fish hold weeks waiting for the right water conditions before migrating upstream. Coho will mix with the chum salmon also waiting to run up-stream, so don't be fooled by their presence, cast the fly to any fish in range, maybe a chum will take your fly. You can be tricked by these coho because they are so close to the shore and in such shallow water. Casting from the beach can be very effective because you will always be in shallow water at the end of your retrieve and that is where the fish are holding. The satisfaction of catching a large coho on a cast fly is great and I recommend it highly.

River Fishing:

River fishing for Coho is popular with the local fishermen. I don't like it. These fish have suffered untold danger to return to spawn, I think that once a salmon reaches its home river it should be safe to spawn. There is no problem catching these fish to eat when they are in the salt water and they are in much better eating condition. The stream fishermen have the Steelhead and Trout to catch in the rivers I think they should leave the Coho alone once they reach fresh water. That's one man's opinion.

For the stream fisherman that wants to try for Coho, the same locations and methods I describe for Steelhead are applicable. Typically the timing for the Coho runs are October and November depend on river water levels. A quick call to any sporting goods store or hotel on the Charlottes will give you the conditions.

Story : Bill Twining

Half the joy of the fishing experience is not the fish but your companions. In the case of Merrill (Bill) Twining, it maybe three quarters of the joy.

Bill Twining is a four star U.S. Marine Corps general (retired) and quite an American hero from the Pacific theatre of WW II (something I was told by others as Bill would never see it that way). His brother was the Chairman of the Joint Chief of Staff (the head of the U.S. military) and the commander of the U.S. Air Force for many years. No simple task for two brothers that started out from simple beginnings.

Bill wanted to come to the Charlottes since 1949, but for some reason or another he didn't make it until 1982. He drove up from California in his Jeep Wagoneer. Bill is an octogenarian but still addicted to the sound and feel of a fish on the end of his line.

I met Bill in the Sandspit Inn and was talked into taking him fishing the next morning. That was the start of a six year adventure in Queen Charlotte Islands fishing. That first day Bill and I went fishing off Sewell Inlet and caught so many coho that Bills' thumbs were sore from the single action fly reel he was not familiar with. The sun burned off the fog and this

September day was fishing Nirvana. That first day has turned into many more, almost all with the same sunny weather and good fishing success.

Bill encouraged the development of my first floating fishing camp, or as his wife called it "a fish trap". (It was not the fish that were trapped.) He encouraged the second camp with a prepayment of his summer guiding fees after the first camp crossed the Hecate Strait in a huge southeasterly. (Thank goodness no one was aboard!)

Bill's undying support and encouragement forced me to fish more than I would have on my own. It is nice to have someone to write to about new sporting accomplishments; no one else understands like Bill does.

With all that fishing there are a number of good anecdotes worth sharing.

The September Labour Day long weekend is a good time to go fishing and the weather is expected to be good. Bill, myself, my wife, Sherry, and my two small children, Richard and Erica all decided to go to Matheson Inlet for the weekend and get in some coho fishing. The fishing as I remember wasn't that great but we caught enough of Bill's favorite eating fish, jack coho.

Everything was going well until the wind came up, but it was September so I didn't worry. That was a mistake. We were anchored in a sheltered bay, and the wind howled heavier as the night grew darker. The roof of the cabin Sherry and the kids were in kept banging and bending, and no one was sleeping. Finally the rain started and I thought the wind would die a bit. Whether it did or not was irrelevant, because at 1:00 am the anchor pulled free and we headed out to sea on a log raft in a small cabin. Luckily the beach line held and we swung onto the beach through the breaking waves.

There we were, inky dark, heavy rain and about seven wet logs with waves breaking over them to navigate before we could reach the safety of terra firma.

As the captain of this event I made the decision to abandon ship and had to try and figure the best way to get everyone to dry land. Bill had a bad knee at the time and needed help to make it to shore, but he would have no part of even moving before Sherry and the kids were safe. So into the surf I went one at a time until all were ashore. Bill was the last to abandon ship and was only concerned for everyone else's welfare.

The only shelter on the beach was a green house the hippies had built a few years before. It had very little plastic left, but was better than nothing. As the tide receded I went aboard the raft to get some blankets and a storm lantern. Once back at the green house we found that the hippies had left more than just plastic. Bill's generation had missed the marijuana craze and he was fascinated with the plant. Finally he clipped a few leaves to show his wife in California and tucked them into his breast pocket. I said, "What if they find them at the border?" and Bill replied "What are they going to do? Throw an eighty year old in jail for two leaves?". He had a good point.

Early the next morning we went aboard the high and dry float with the cabin on a 40 degree list. At high tide that morning, I towed the float into a better anchorage. We found out later that the wind blew 72 knots that night, that is over 90 miles per hour.

That was the most exciting time I had in South Moresby as far as life and limb were concerned but there are some good fishing stories also.

Juan Perez Sound is always serving up a new experience for those of us that spend any time there. The Dahls propoise are ready to chase any boat cutting in and out of the bow wave close enough for a fishermen to touch them as they dart by. Schools of coho are always present and will take to attacking anything silver. My Boston Whaler has a chrome cover on the bottom of the self bailing hole, and is hit by these revved up cohos.

Bill and I discovered many hot fishing spots along with his son David. Needle fish seemed to be the preferred prey for these lively cohos and we gathered them live from the beach where they spawn in the gravel at the waters edge.

Without live bait we fish three lines with different flies on each line. I hold one rod in my hand and one across my legs and steer with the other hand while Bill holds his own rod. Usually I catch a fish on one rod and hand the other one to Bill to hold while I play the first one. He immediately gets two strikes and two fish on, now what? One way or another we lose one or two fish and boat one with more laughter and confusion than a Chevy Chase movie.

The right fishing partner is usually more important than the fishing itself, at least that is true of Bill Twining.

Story : My Dream

Those of us who like fishing, make that, who are addicted to fishing, have always wanted to own a fishing camp somewhere in the wilds of British Columbia. Most are smart enough to only want such a thing. I on the other hand, had one.

Fish camps, as they are called, are places to relax, drink a beer, and catch fish at will, on calm sun lit days. Places that you invite your friends to join you and entertain fishing clients to help pay the bills. Camps are the romantic legends of our outdoor heritage. I've read of many such places on French sounding rivers back east and in the North West Territories.

When I moved to the Queen Charlotte Islands I thought it was the perfect place for such a camp. I already had two Boston Whalers and a good understanding of the fish on the Charlottes, what else could I need?

South Moresby was the right place, pristine wilderness, unfished, available. I knew from past experience that Juan Perez was the perfect area to fish. It even had tubs of hot water at Hot Springs Island.

I spent a summer investigating the fishing and found it great, coho on every beach, strong sea-going fish that would test any fisherman's desire. I was determined, more than ever to have a camp.

Matheson Inlet is on the south side of Juan Perez Sound and was the site of some unobtrusive hand logging by a French logger named Andre Quirielle. He had a float with a cabin anchored in the inlet and was finished logging. I had my chance, and for a few thousand dollars I had my fish camp. That was the beginning of an episode that spanned four summers.

The first year things went relatively well until we realized that there were others that called the inlet and the cabin I just bought, home. Hippies is the nice term. I arrived in Matheson Inlet a few days ahead of some fishing guests, only to find two people living (and drying seaweed and halibut) in my cabin,with their boat tied up to my float. Never mind the junk on the float in addition to the goat and its droppings. It seemed that he thought the Frenchman had promised to sell him the cabin and float a year earlier, even though no money had changed hands. He wouldn't leave so I untied the float and moved down the inlet to a new anchorage. That afternoon the wind came up and we were dragging anchor so we headed back to the original location and there we stayed, goat and all.

Our friends with the goat were also in charge of the green house on the beach that housed some suspicious looking plants. More on that later.

We had worked out a truce of sorts when the second boat arrived. This skipper thought the world was near anarchy and had his survival rations and assorted armaments including handguns, semi-automatic shotguns, and much amunition,to fend off wouldbe attackers. You must remember, we are 70 miles by water to the closest road, and then 40 minutes by truck to a community of only 500 people. This is the quiet wilderness that the environmentalists want preserved?

We agreed to disagree on the public-ness of my float and were stuck with them for the first fishing trip. The fishermen thought these guys were cartoon characters and saw it as a great laugh. I was not impressed.

The next thing was a surprise air raid from the Prince Rupert Royal Canadian Police in their Grumman Goose aircraft. They circled so long that by the time the aircraft landed the plants were scattered in the bushes by our friends. Boats, cabins and persons are all searched with little of anything accomplished. Here we are in the pristine wilderness and my property is being searched for drugs! I have never so much as had a cop look in my car before. Maybe there is more to operating a fish camp than meets the eye!

That summer ended without any further catastrophic events, save and except for a couple of 50 knot blows, and the rescue of one of Trans Provincial's Beaver aircraft lost in the fog in Juan Perez Sound. At least they ended happily.

Next spring I had an agreement with the uninvited guests that they would stay away during the summer while I was fishing. I thought I would go down to the cabin early just in case.

This time we had a new friend in my cabin. He was the same type, took a swim every day in the 50 degree water, never wore clothes unless it was snowing, and slept with an eighty pound Russian wolf hound he trained to kill deer. This one had no boat, and had hitched a ride with a fish boat which let him off first chance, I'm sure. He too had goats, a ewe and a kid. I'll say one thing for this fellow, he would do anything for his animals.

One day the local bear decided to have the kid goat for lunch and was well on his way through the first course when our friend attacked him with a stick the size of a thin baseball bat. The bear took a couple of shots in head and finally gave up the remains of the kid goat, which our hippie promptly made into a stew. I would not take on a large black bear with a stick just for a dead goat, but then I wear clothes when it is cold, too!

We had to supply this one with construction material so he

would move as far away from the float as possible. He grew on us and by the end of the summer we supplied him with a free airplane ride to Sandspit and a friend spotted him the money to go to Toronto for his daughter's birthday. He may still be there. We never heard from him again.

While all this was going on, Western Forest Products helicoptered in one day with the forest service, to explain the need for a crown lease for the green house on the beach and the new building on the point. I just laughed and told them to see the naked guy down the beach, and we all had a good laugh.

I could go on but I think you have the message. The first camp, of two log rafts and three small buildings, drifted across Hecate Strait the next spring during a 75 knot storm and was never seen again.

My 15 foot Boston Whaler was on the deck of that float when it went to sea, and I wrote it off as lost. That summer I started looking for a replacement and phoned M&P Marine in Vancouver, the Whaler dealer for B.C.

The salesman asked some questions about my last boat, and after a short conversation said, "I can sell you a new whaler, but it would be easier for you to pick up your old one". The phone went dead as I tried to understand what he had said.

The R.C.M.P. were trying to track down the owner of a 15 foot Boston Whaler picked up by a commercial fish boat at Freman Pass 30 miles southeast of Prince Rupert. My skiff had crossed Hecate Strait 100 miles due north of Juan Perez Sound, where it started. The commercial fisherman put the skiff on deck and took it to Vancouver for safekeeping.

When found, the whaler had everything in place, as if the owner had just fallen overboard. Except for some cosmetic damage to the hull, caused by being washed off the deck of the float, the skiff was in perfect condition. It was not even full of water, because of its self bailing capacity when empty. Seats, fuel tanks, paddles, everything the way I left them a few weeks earlier.

An incredible testimonial to the seaworthiness and toughness of the Boston Whaler!

We rebuilt, and two years later the second cabin blew off the float, while tied up in Gordon Cove, Moresby Camp. There are no plans for any further fish camps, although I do get the disgusting urge now and again.

Chum Salmon

Life Cycle ○ Catch Methods & Locations

Life Cycle :

The Chum or Dog salmon is the latest to run to its home stream. In the Queen Charlotte Islands this is usually October or later. These fish are the ones that become vertically striped purple and a dull yellow as they mature sexually, readying for spawning. Chums are very silver and bright when they are in the open ocean and are both handsome and lively. Those fishermen that have caught chum in this condition say they are real fighters. The few I've caught in the Charlotte estuaries have proven that even though they were in their striped colouring.

Chums and Pinks follow the same life cycle for the most part although Chums do not have an on and off year like Pinks.

Both Chums and Pinks migrate almost immediately to salt water once they hatch from the stream bottom gravel. This means they are less susceptible to water flow and other stream conditions to survive. Although not proven, the Chum and Pink are thought to be sensitive to estuarine environment where they spend some portion of their first year of life.

Knowledge of this does not directly help catch these species but it does help us to understand the timing of the presence of searun Cutthroat Trout and Dolly Varden Char in Charlotte rivers. Both these aggressive predators devour many newly emerged Pink and Chum salmon fingerlings. No wonder the tied down minnow works so well for these trout! More about that in the trout section.

Catch Methods & Locations :

Chum salmon have not been sports fished successfully enough on the Queen Charlottes to give any real definitive advice. I will list some of the rivers and streams that have runs of Chum accessible by road and worth some experimentation. The really valuable information will be where to intercept these Salmon when they are in the silver bright open ocean condition. I'm working on it and so should you.

Chum Salmon run to Pallant Creek, Yakoun River, and a number of small streams in Skidegate Inlet. These are all worthy of continued investigation.

Campbell River fishermen have been successful with Chums in Deepwater Bay north of the Seymor Narrows, with mooching gear and cut-plug herring for bait. This may work at Langara Island or a similar spot where silver chums can be intercepted.

Commercial trollers have also had success catching some open ocean Chums but this practice has been frowned upon by the federal fisheries department. I think over the next five years sport fishermen will come to understand enough about the Chum Salmon that we will be able to add this silver beauty to our highly prized list of sought-after species.

Sockeye Salmon

Life Cycle • Catch Possibilities & Locations

Life Cycle :

The Sockeye Salmon only resides on the Queen Charlotte Islands as the "creek run" variety. This race of Sockeye Salmon only reaches 3 to 4 pounds and returns to a few streams that are lake-headed, such as the Copper and Yakoun Rivers and Mathers Creek.

The Haida Indians gillnet these fish, as they are excellent eating. The run usually migrates upstream from tidewater in early spring (April, May) and spawn in the fall in tributaries of the lakes that head these rivers, having spent the summer in the headwater lakes.

Catch Possibilities & Locations :

I have tried with no success to catch these fish in the estuaries as they first run upstream. I tried every cast fly I had but no luck. In Alaska the Sockeye will take a fly (pink) in the estuaries and rivers. I leave it to a smarter fishermen than I to figure out that one.

The Sockeye present no real opportunity for the sports fishermen on the Charlottes except as I mentioned earlier, and the possibility of again intercepting these fish at Langara Island bound for the Skeena and Nass Rivers. These fish are very fresh and silver. I leave that to the Langara fish camps to research. The commercial troll fleet has been harvesting Sockeye Salmon, so I think the sports fisherman will also soon discover effective methods for their capture.

Pink Salmon

Life Cycle • Catch Methods & Locations

Life Cycle :

The life cycle of the Pink Salmon is the same as the other salmon species, except for a few minor variations of interest to the angler. Pinks hatch from the gravel, travel to the ocean, spend some years in the ocean and then return to their natal stream to spawn and complete the cycle. Pinks spawn every other year in the Charlottes with one year being the high year and very few returning the next. The Queen Charlotte Island Pink fisherman needs to know which streams are productive on which years. The even years are the large return years for the Charlotte streams. 1990, 1992, 1994 etc. will be the best for Pinks.

Catch Methods & Locations :

To catch these hard fighting fish, you must intercept them before they are too close to their natal stream. The reasons for this are: the fish become less suitable for the table, and less likely to take any type of terminal gear the closer they come to their home stream. The fisherman should attempt to catch these fish when they are schooled up, but not yet close to the home stream.

Examples of this strategy are the fishery in Darwin Sound in South Moresby during July when the schooling pinks can be taken with a small cast spinner or a trolled red hoochie, with or without spinner in front. Pinks school off the Sandspit Bar prior to the run to the Copper River and streams in Skidegate Inlet. Some success has been had with standard flasher gear, but like the Coho, the Pink deserve a lighter tackle fate.

The Yakoun River has some incredibly large runs of Pink salmon. 1988 was expected to be very large, to the sports angler a real chance to try some new and innovative methods to catch this overlooked species.

Remember that Pinks are not fair game once they reach fresh water, according to fisheries regulations, (not that they're worth the pursuit into fresh water anyway).

Masset Inlet and off the mouth of Masset Inlet can be excellent places to intercept Pinks either running to streams in Masset Inlet itself or possibly the runs to the Skeena and Nass Rivers, as they migrate through Dixon Entrance.

Pinks are not large salmon, and therefore I recommend you catch them with a number 7-8-9 flyrod, 200 yards of monofilament backed with dacron line on your regular flyreel, and terminated with no more than 2 ounces of weight (most times with 5/8 of an ounce keel weights) and a red hoochie, bucktail, or flashtail with a small spinner (abalone or silver) in front. Or cast to them with a small spinner (yellow maybe) with light spinning gear. On light tackle these little guys can give a good account of themselves and make some very good eating or smoking.

One note of caution, if you are going to fish with your trout or non salt water flyreel then be prepared to wash them out and dry them after each day fishing. I am going to design and produce an all stainless steel single action flyreel one day, for just this type of fishing, but until then keep the salt away from your precious reels.

I have not indicated areas on the charts for Pink fishing, but I will list the rivers and streams that I think will produce catchable Pinks on the even years when the returns are large.

The Yakoun River run is the best bet any even year, with the Copper River, Pallant Creek, and small streams in Skidegate Inlet, including the Deena River for closewater easy to get to. Naden Harbour, Darwin Sound, Cumshewa Inlet and Sewell Point as areas where the fishing should be good but have much more difficult access.

Section : **Steelhead**

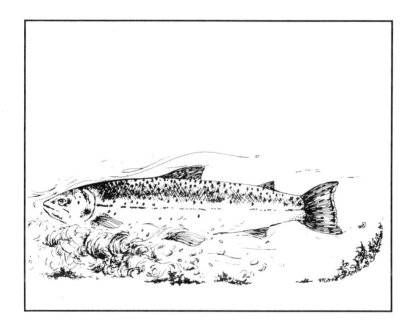

Story : President Jimmy Carter

From time to time the small community of Sandspit gets a feeling for the life of a big city. The time Jimmy Carter, ex-President of the United States came to go steelhead fishing was one of those times.

Ex-Presidents of the United States are all under heavy security until their last breath, so in addition to President Carter, his fishing party and his famous wife, there were 16 secret service bodyguards and because they were in Canada, 16 Royal Canadian Policemen came along to keep an eye on the Americans.

The President and his party, three other fishermen and his wife Rosalyn, were in Sandspit to fish for steelhead at the beginning of April. They fished the Deena River where Richard Osborne and I were also fishing for the day. We met the President's party at the Deena West bridge and to show some good Queen Charlotte Islands hospitality, I offered the party a few of the wool flies that I designed specially for the Deena River.

Richard and I fished downstream and then back to the bridge with one fish taken by Richard and a few more hits. We reached the bridge as one of the members of the President's party arrived and immediately requested more of my flies because everyone had lost theirs. He said the president had been using a "Skykomish Sunrise" with no luck and upon trying on my fly had one fish and more hits before losing the fly on the bottom.

He had also had good luck with my flies and wanted two dozen more if I had them and would pay handsomely. I had only 5 or 6 in my fly card so I offered them to him and said I could tie some more tonight. Great! and off he went up-stream.

I headed for the Six Mile Hole and arrived to see two steelhead laying in the two foot deep tailout water in plain view. I spent an hour trying to entice these fish to take, including almost hitting them with a fly, but no luck, they were interested in more amorous activities. A different fisherman from the president's party arrived and we fished together for another hour and had a good chat. It seems that this fellow had fished the Charlottes before and had played a part in bringing the President to the Charlottes. He also told me some fishing stories about this particular trip that are fun to share.

It seems that anywhere President Carter goes, his secret service bodyguards go, complete with Uzi machine guns in their day packs. On this particular day the President was fishing the same Six Mile Hole on the Deena River, President on one side and the friend recounting the story on the opposite side of the river. On the Charlottes there are many old trees that are ready to fall because of rot, and on this particular occasion a large branchless snag decided to fall about 20 feet from the President. The president's friend telling the story saw the snag was going to miss the President so he said nothing. The president and his bodyguard were facing the other way with the bodyguard just leaning up against an alder tree for a nap, when this snag crashed to the ground with the sound of an explosion. No need to say that the bodyguard had his gun out and needed a change of underwear. In a moment everyone was laughing.

Sandspit was a busy spot while the Carters were in town. Frank Beban showed the President and his party some great hospitality with a complete helicopter tour of South Moresby, only to have Jimmy support the National Park and help put

Frank out of business. I tied the two dozen flies that night, took me until 10:30 to finish, and delivered them to where the party was staying only to be impolitely dismissed at the door by the proprietor. They got my flies but I never received so much as a thank you. I guess being President means you can suspend common courtesy.

There were rumours that the President and his wife used roe when they became frustrated with not catching steelhead with a straight fly but I hope that this is not true, since President Carter has been represented as the real true flyfishing purist.

Steelhead Trout

Preface:

Steelhead fishing on the Queen Charlottes has a very large reputation. Most of it is warranted. To many fishermen the Steelhead is the premier west coast game fish. To others, it ranks among the bone fish, and tarpon, for fishing action.

My good friend Marty Bowles came to the Charlottes to catch steelhead on his new fly-rod and reel. We drove to Pallant Creek to test our luck . Marty wanted to catch a good steelhead on a fly and had a brand new sinking fly line to try. I tied on one of my pink wool flies to give one particular beat a thorough-going investigation. I can't remember how many casts Marty made but he had soon witnessed the white maw of an aggressive steelhead, but had not hooked him. A few casts later I heard the expected shout of a friend with a fish well hooked.

I think Marty was more surprised than anything else. He had lots of experience catching the high jumping coho of South Moresby, but a good steelhead in fast running water was another story.

The run we were fishing has a 90 degree upstream turn and a 70 foot tree and stump half submerged along the far bank. The water is 12 feet deep along the tree, and shallows out into a wide 4 foot deep tailout with boulders and a downed alder tree. From the head water to the out flow over a 4 foot falls, the run is probably 250 feet long and 40 feet wide, but one of the best and most consistent beats on Pallant Creek

Marty's steelhead immediately made a 3 foot jump and ran upstream around the corner. I figured we had lost him for sure. Not so. The fish rested for 10 seconds and came screaming downstream right under the half submerged tree on the far bank,- lost for sure this time. So sure was I, that I had even given up shouting instructions. Marty wasn't giving up and after another 20 seconds he coached the fish back to playable water, this time the fish went upstream but not around the corner, and held. Marty put some pressure on, but no budging this brute. It was then that I told Marty that he was in good shape, because as long as the fish didn't run downstream, he should land him. Bad comment. I think the steelhead heard me, because he immediately turned downstream and ripped Marty's complete fly line off his reel, and was gone over the falls. The line broke at the backing knot - Marty had just lost his brand new flyline.

He didn't speak for a while, just contemplated the universe. I was glad we had not brought our deer rifles because it could have been a dangerous time for me. It really is human nature to look for the reason you lost that fish, especially the reasons that had nothing to do with you.

I gained a tremendous respect for Marty that day. After a while he quietly smiled and said,"Boy that was one hell of a steelhead! "" I'll second that," I said.

We still talk about the fish Marty lost, like it was 20 minutes ago. I can't tell you how the last steelhead I caught fought, but I will never forget the one Marty lost. Maybe that's why everyone makes such a big deal about this sea-run trout.

Life Cycle :

Steelhead are really a sea run trout, but they act more like a salmon it terms of their life cycle. Some Queen Charlotte Steelhead start life in the streams that feed a lake that in turn feeds another stream that outflows to the ocean. Others spawn in the main stem of the major rivers throughout the Charlottes. Most steelhead holding streams on the Charlottes are lake headed, the Yakoun River , the Copper River, Pallant Creek, and many others. Other streams that have good summer holding water also rear steelhead. When I am looking for a new river to try for Steelhead I always look to the headwaters to determine if the river's flow can be ameliorated and guaranteed by the presence of a lake. This same lake will also give the steelhead preferred spawning habitat in its small inflow streams.

Once the Steelhead starts life in the gravel of the stream bed, he is subject to many stream side predators before he migrates to sea. Some Steelhead migrate the next spring to the ocean and spend 1 to 3 years there before returning. The majority remain in their natal streams for 2 years and then migrate downstream to the ocean to complete the sea-run phase.

The Steelhead's whereabouts are not well understood while in the ocean. Most experts think that the Steelhead spends from 1 to 3 years in the ocean somewhere in the North Pacific. These fish return to spawn once for the most part, but in smaller numbers, twice. There is even a suggestion that a few Queen Charlotte Island Steelhead actually spawn more than twice, but this remains to be confirmed.

Along the road to Moresby camp there are a number of small streams, more like ditches, that Steelhead spawn in. These fish can be watched, paired up holding or actively spawning, usually under some overgrowth of salmon berry bush or alder trees. These mates are now dark red, males with a hooked jaw, and females not as pronouncedly changed. The male will soon descend the river to expend his life in the ocean, the female will do the same but may return to spawn again. The female has laid approximately 10,000 eggs and will be pleased if 10 adult Steelhead return to spawn in 4 to 5 years time. To watch this precious event, gives the fisherman a keen sense of nature's cycle and may induce an additional release of a healthy steelhead in the angling years ahead.

Steelhead and the Coho salmon are two species that spend some time rearing in their natal stream and subsequently have distinct characteristics for stream feeding during this stream resident period. This information should help the angler predict some of the returning Steelhead's behaviour. Steelhead are aggressive fish, and will take many types of terminal gear under many different water conditions. I think this trait must have something to do with the Steelheads fresh water experience as a parr. Spawning Steelhead like to hold in certain positions in any given river, this is also true of parr Steelhead. Charlotte rivers have beats that include many headwater holding spots, these locations are only effectively fished with float equipped fishing gear, more on fishing gear later.

Defining River Terms :

Four terms need to be defined so that I can explain some of the more common holding areas for the Charlotte Steelhead.

Headwaters are the beginnings of any run, usually with fast flows, and are immediately downstream of the last upstream tailout.

Tailouts are the waters that shallow up at the downstream end of a run of water. **Slot water** is the water, usually in the centre of the run, that is narrow and deeper than the surrounding water. Slot water is usually faster than normal flows. The fourth term is **back water**, water that is slower than the normal flow and usually deeper, with nothing to show at the surface what the water is doing below the surface.

Certain types of fishing techniques are more effective than others given the majority of the water type on each river. I will attempt to suggest the specific river to the type of fishing techniques most effective.

Fishing Methods:

There are four major types of Steelhead fishing techniques used on the Charlottes: **Float, Bottom bouncing, Fly fishing, and Spin casting.** All these methods are used but the first three are the most common. I have exclusively fished with a fly for the last four years. Although this method has somewhat limited the runs that I can effectively fish the trade off has been well worth the extra satisfaction of catching and playing a Steelhead on fly rod and line.

Float fishing for Steelhead with a single action reel of the Silex type is a well established tradition on the British Columbia coast. The short fast flow streams of the rugged coastline of B.C. are fished very effectively with the float method. Using a 8 to 10 foot, fairly stiff rod, one attaches a swivel (two or three way) and then approximately 30 inches of leader(10, 12, 15 pound). The leader is weighted with spit shots, foil lead or similar material, evenly along the leader. A float made of cork or plastic, is attached to the mainline (15, 18, or 20 pounds) and can slide up or down the line, but not without substantial force being exerted on the float. This way the terminal gear can be adjusted to the depth of the water by raising or lowering the float. This fishing arrangement is cast side arm and with practice, can be cast very accurately with a minimum of backcasting room. The single action reel will free spool line so that the float and bait can be drifted downstream without drag that would cause the terminal gear to rise in the water column. The leader and terminal gear(usually roe or an artificial imitation roe) can be fished just off the bottom, but directly below the float. This float. This method makes fishing small slot waters and areas of much bottom organic debris easier than any other methods.

In the Charlottes the Copper and Tlell Rivers are known for their many sunken branches and logs and their productive backwaters. Float fishing these rivers is the best method for productive fishing.

Bottom bouncing is a more American method, probably arriving here with the first Washington State fishermen. This method uses the same rod and line, but usually is teamed with a level wind reel of the Ambassador type. Same mainline (without the float) and leader, sometimes without the swivel (just a blood knot), as with float fishing. This gear type uses less weight, but the same terminal gear. The line is cast quartering upstream and fished bouncing lightly on the bottom through 120 degrees. Needless to say, with bottom obstructions this method is very frustrating. Rivers such as the Yakoun, Deena, and Mamin are best suited to bottom bouncing.

Classic fly fishing water is not that plentiful. Since there are no summer run Steelhead there are no fish willing to take a dry fly, so the majority of the fly fishing is wet fly. (Tasu Sound streams are reputed to have summer run Steelhead, but I have never found a witness to this fact). Also Tasu is a difficult place to get to.

Wet fly fishing is done with either a fast sinking line, a line with a fast sinking tip (10 feet) or a floater with a sinking piece attached or a fast sinking shooting head. I have used all these types and now use a straight floater with a ten foot fast sinking head and a very short leader (20 inches). This line is a monster to cast , but most casts are roll casts anyway, the Charlottes having very few backcasts except on the Yakoun River. In high flows and on many runs the fisherman needs a split shot to get down to the fish. I know this may be sacrilege to some purists but these fish will not consistently come up in the water column to take a fly that is not presented on their nose.

The fly type used in the Charlottes is varied, wool flies of the orange, red, green and black are very effective. I think presentation of the fly to the Steelhead is far more important than the fly pattern, but I may be proved wrong in the future. Dean River patterns and Kispiox flies are used here to good advantage.

As previously stated, Jimmy Carter, ex-President of the United States, fished the Charlottes with some of my wool fly patterns and found good success, when his own patterns were not producing. I am not sure if this was just presentation or the flies, but his fishing partners swore than it was the wool flies that did the trick.

The last fishing method that needs some discussion is **Spin casting**. Although not many Steelhead fishermen spin cast on the Charlottes, this is a very effective fishing method. Using small spinners or spoons for terminal gear, aggressive Steelhead will charge these attractors. Neophyte fishermen can master the spinning rod faster than other methods and therefore can have more fun in a shorter period of time. Any terminal gear from float, bottom bouncing, and even fishing with a fly can be accommodated with spinning gear.

That rounds out the fishing methods for Steelhead on the Queen Charlotte Islands.

I present no information on hooks or other terminal tackle because there is no real consensus on a particular "Queen Charlotte" Steelhead tackle and others have done an excellent job on describing this aspect of the sport. Most terminal tackle from gooey-bobs, to corkies, to just plain wool of different colours, works very well to entice Steelhead.

Steelhead Rivers :
Yakoun River:

The premier Steelhead river, and the largest on the Charlottes' is the Yakoun River. The Yakoun has been producing the largest Steelhead caught on the Islands for many years. Twenty-plus pound fish are caught on the Yakoun every year.

The season extends from November to May with runs of large fish in November and March. The Yakoun itself hosts all species of salmon including a small protected run of Spring salmon, trout, (sea-run cutthroat and dolly varden char),and the Steelhead trout. There may be some resident rainbow trout but I suspect these fish are pre-migrant Steelhead.

The Yakoun River has a very large watershed with a headwater at Yakoun Lake. The River is closed above the Fishing Boundary sign about 32 kilometres from the Queen Charlotte City log dump (just at the 32 orange road sign) and therefore, at least one half of the river is left to the Steelhead for unfettered spawning. I feel that much more spawning takes place in the tributaries that flow into Yakoun Lake than is recognized; however the lower half of the river is a large enough area for even the most ambitious angler.

MacMillan Bloedel has been logging in the Yakoun watershed for many years and is committed to protect fish stocks in the river. The network of logging roads, active and dormant, has made access to the river very convenient. This easy access will probably be the biggest detriment to the Steelhead stocks on the Yakoun. As the example on Vancouver Island shows, the real threat to our Steelhead stocks is over-killing. Easy access is always the first pre-requisite for a decline in any sports fish stock.

I hope that to the benefit of both the Steelhead and the Cutthroat trout that the Ministry of Environment will see fit to ban the use of roe on the Yakoun River. The aggressive Steelhead on the Yakoun can be caught easily without roe, therefore I see no need to encourage the killing of the important female steelhead for their roe. Many more fish are mortally hooked with roe than other terminal gear because it is taken so deeply by both cutthroat and Steelhead. Over the years the incidental kill of the sea-run cutthroat has been high, this waste would be reduced if roe is banned, as it is on many other rivers in British Columbia.

The Yakoun River is made up of a number of different sections, most of the good water is wide (100 feet) and is adaptable to bottom bouncing (clean bottom) or fly fishing (some backcast). This river is large enough to have every type of fishable water, the tailouts on some of the more popular holes can be fished with a fly with good results ("40Q" bridge for example). Floating the river in a small rubber raft is also popular. That way you can access the runs that take a long walk in from the road on the downstream sections. The Yakoun can supply many good slot water runs and some effective backwaters, where roe is the traditional bait. I enjoy the large and diverse tailouts with a fly. Fishing this large river is seldom very crowded, although you will see other fishermen. If this bothers you just go up or downstream a few hundred yards and you will be alone again.

Enclosed in the body of this book is an updated map of the Yakoun River and its logging road access. **Remember the logging roads that you will travel on are private. You must check in with either the MacMillan Bloedel Juskatla Office or the Queen Charlotte City shop for clearance. Your life depends on it!** You will likely receive friendly advice as to the fishing on the Yakoun by some of the employees.

Yakoun River Directions:

I will describe how to get to some of the more commonly fished areas, but this is by no means the total body of information on the Yakoun.

There are two directions to access the Yakoun River, by the south from Queen Charlotte City or the North through Port Clements.

Access through Queen Charlotte City: The trip to fishable water is about 35 kilometres. Start by driving to the western end of Queen Charlotte City where you arrive at the MacMillan Bloedel shop and a logging road on your right. During working hours, you must proceed to the shop for someone to clear you to your destination. Once cleared you will receive two maps of the road network. (You already have the one in this book, but in years to come the shop maps will be updated). Travel north on the mainline, probably following a logging truck, until you cross a bridge at 22kilometre sign (orange on this section). This is the top end of the Yakoun River and is closed to fishing usually from October to May. Check the sports fishing regulations for details. You will pass a sign that says Port Clements or Juskatla, stay right, headed to Port Clements. Continue on past the 30 k sign(orange) until you see the river again on the right. About 32 kilometres is the Fishing Boundary sign on the edge of the river. Start fishing from here downstream. There are numerous old stub roads that go down to the water's edge on your right for the next ten kilometres or so. Just after you pass the "King" sign the kilometre signs change to red and you will notice that the numbers decrease as you go North.

There is a canyon section along this stretch of river that I have taken a canoe down and had some fun. There are log jams and the like, so scout the river out before you try anything. Remember the river changes every year.

One of the most productive areas of the Yakoun is the area around the '40Q' bridge. If you continue north on the mainline as you were you come to a sharp left bend in the road with a road going right, make this sharp right turn and take the first right to the '40Q' bridge, it is only a kilometre or so from the turn. You know you are on the right road when you see the Memorial to one of our fallen fishermen. If you see the City Resources sign on another road to the sharp right you went too far, turn around and go back. Once you have turned off the mainline to go to the bridge you can continue down river by just going straight ahead instead of taking the first right. Downstream there are more stubs on the right that lead to the river.

If you are coming from Port Clements, start by driving through Port toward Juskatla. Drive approximetaly 18 kilometres to the Juskatla turn off (see the signs) and proceed to the Juskatla Office during office hours, or continue on the mainline another 25 kilometres past the Marie Lake Fish Hatchery (on the right) and past the 27 k red sign bearing right at the City Resouces sign and straight ahead at the sharp right hand bend, taking the first right to the '40Q' bridge or continuing downstream by staying straight ahead. The rest of the river can be explained by reading the explanation of the route from Queen Charlotte backwards. It sounds difficult but when you are there it is easy.

Exploring, by hiking or rafting this tremendous river, will grant you your own secrets places where the "giants hold". I wish you hard lines and dry waders.

The Tlell River:

The Tlell River flows north from the Pontoons (a swampy lake in the central part of southeast Graham Island) to its out flow at Tlell on the east coast of Graham Island. The Tlell River Bridge is the best landmark for the river, just north of Naikoon Provincial Park Headquarters.

The Tlell is another tea-coloured river about the size of the Copper River. In fact the Tlell has many similarities with the Copper River. They are both difficult to find backcast and have considerable debris on the bottom.

Timing for the Tlell River starts in February and goes through April. The fish can be large, but 18 pounds is uncommon with the 10 to 12 pounders being talked about.

The weather can effect the Tlell because the Pontoons is not really a lake, but rather a swamp area that is flooded by a few days of heavy rain. Colour is not usually the problem if the river is in flood, but high water makes the river even harder to fish effectively.

To access this river you can start at the bridge on the main highway and turn right just before you enter the bridge and drive down Beitush Road which runs along the river almost to tidewater. This area holds the Coho in the fall and searun cutthroats in the spring, however the Steelhead are usually on the upstream sections of the river.

You can turn left coming north just before you reach the Richardson Ranch down Wiggins Road to the end and walk to the river to fish up or downstream. Again there is a trail which follows the river that can be accessed along the main highway opposite the "Tlell Unincorporated" sign about 2 kilometres south of Wiggins Road. Watch out for the cattle and make sure you close any gates that you open, and obey the signs. Let's keep the fisherman's good reputation intact.

Fishing the Tlell can be best done with the float fishing arrangement so that you can get your terminal gear down to the the fish in the many slot water spots.

Walking is the order of the day when it comes to fishing the Tlell and the further you walk upstream the more unfished water there is. I have flown down the Tlell from the Pontoons many times in my small plane and marvel at the water on the Tlell that is sparsely fished. From the air it looks like one could hike all the way into the headwater along the river, but it always looks easier from the air. This difficult access will always give the fish a chance to spawn in peace further upriver and maybe that is a good thing.

Copper River :
The Copper River outflows into Copper Bay (10 kilometres south of Sandspit on the Copper Bay Mainline). The river and mainline follow the valley south, the road bridging the river in

two places.

The Copper is a tea-coloured river, most famous for its large coho salmon. Steelhead fishing on the Copper starts in December and continues through April, with the Christmas run the most fished. I have had some superb fishing on Boxing day over the years. The Copper produces a few large fish (18 pounds) but many 10 to 12 pound healthy fish.

The river is tight to fish. That means many overhanging branches, and few open runs with any backcast space. The bottom of the river is very debris laden therefore it is not a river to bottom bounce. Float fishing is very effective because of the rivers many slot waters and obstructions. I find fly fishing is difficult to have fun with on the Copper and I concentrate on other rivers. The Copper, because it is close to Sandspit can receive some fishing pressure during periods of good fishing. Simply fishing other rivers on the weekends will usually free up the Copper during the week, when the locals are working.

The Copper River can be affected by the weather, even though the river is lake headed. This river will be in the trees after two or three days of good rain, if the ground is already wet (it usually is at this time of the year).

High flows are usually clear enough to fish but not practical. When the Copper is in the trees that is a literal statement, and unless you can cast from a branch it is better to go to another river.

To fish the Copper, the fisherman either starts at the upstream end, the second bridge, and fishes down, or he can start at the 18 kilometre sign and walk east down to the river following the trail and fish upstream. Most local fishermen drive from fishing location to fishing location along the mainline. Steelhead hold at certain locations in the river, and they are all marked by obvious pull off spots in the road. I have located the more well known fishing holes on the map, but the best way to fish the Copper is to try the likely looking water.

Deena River:

The Deena River is located west of Sandspit about 30 kilometres on the paved road to Alliford Bay Ferry and then on the gravel along the Alliford Bay mainline to South Bay where you should either check with the Crown Forest operation or follow a logging vehicle. You continue west along the Deena mainline until you reach the river (obvious because of the estuary you will see on your right). The gravel road is rough in spots but remember it wasn't built for recreation, it's a working road built to keep this province's standard of living high.

The Deena River is a lovely stream, with a good clean bottom and some room to maneuver your fishing rod. Again Crown Forest has followed the river with the Deena Main and Deena West Main logging roads. Access has been improved greatly by this. The Deena is an open river with a valley bottom that has fairly old alder trees , having been logged quite a few years ago. This mix of old alder trees and good coastal blacktail deer populations have kept the river side relatively clear of under-brush making walking up and downstream very enjoyable.

Timing for the Deena River is later than the Copper River, it begins in March and peaks in April with some fish in May. The Deena seems more affected by weather than most streams because it is not lake headed. The Deena can go out in terms of colour easily with a good spring storm involving a good two days of rain on saturated soil. Prolonged heavy rain floods the Deena and causes it to be unfishable for a few days, but it will clear quickly once the rain has stopped.

I recommend fishing this river by walking along the bank and fishing all good looking water. Start at the river outflow, at the height of tidal influence (same as the tide water sign posted by federal fisheries department) and fish upstream to the first bridge where the Deena West main starts. Pay close attention to the first long slot water run a few hundred yards from where

74

you started. This run produces many coho in the fall besides very fresh Steelhead in March and April. End this walk at probably the most consistent producing pool on the Deena; the bridge pool, under the Deena West bridge.

The second walk starts at the first turn off on the right once you pass by the bridge staying on the Deena Main. It is a short walk to the river, and you can walk downstream to the bridge and fish a few good runs, or fish upstream quite a way to the next major holding pool, called the Six Mile Hole. Access the Six Mile Hole directly, by crossing the bridge and proceed up the Deena West Main, bearing left at the first major intersection. The trail down to the Six Mile Hole is a little difficult because of alder tree suppression a few years ago, but it is worth the trouble. From the bridge it is 2.2 kilometres. This pool is where I hooked one of the few Steelhead that came to a surface fly, or make that a wet fly that was surfing. A beautiful 12 pound doe that had been tagged two years before and must have been returning for her second spawning. Quite the fish, and one I just had to release to keep those genes alive.

Good fishing can be experienced from the Six Mile Hole upstream but I am usually fished out by the time I arrive. So I will leave the rest of the river to your exploration. The water is there, it just needs the desire.

For me the Deena is one of the nicest rivers to fly fish on the Charlottes, but any gear type will work. The river has slot water, and back waters for float fishing and good clean bottom for bottom bouncing.

Pallant Creek :

Pallant Creek flows into Cumshewa Inlet at Moresby Camp and is a forty minute drive form Sandspit. By far the best way to travel to the Pallant is to drive to South Bay the same as you would going to the Deena River. Again, check with the Crown

Forest operations or follow a logging truck left up the hill one kilometre west of South Bay and proceed 6 kilometres to the Moresby road. Turn right and travel approximately 7 kilometres to the Pallant Creek Fish Hatchery, a good place to start!

The Pallant is a pretty little stream that starts in Mosquito Lake, (the namesake for the World War II bomber because the spruce trees that were used to construct these aircraft were logged from this lake) and flows through a number of canyons and steep gradients. The Pallant is my favorite Charlotte Steelhead stream, although it is not classic fly water, there are a few perfect beats for the fly. The drive keeps the fishermen to a minimum also.

One of the tricks to fishing the Pallant is not to let the hatchery staff know you are on the river because they are notorious at driving to the next pool and fishing the water in front of you. I always fish to the hatchery, that way they don't know you are there until you are finished for the day. This lack of fishing etiquette is not normal but for some reason the government's servants of the people think they have a special position with the Pallant Creek. Make sure you visit the hatchery and see how your millions of dollars have been spent.

The Pallant does not have large fish, although a few 18 pounders have been taken. The Steelhead tend to be in the 10 pound class and are good strong fighters. The run of Steelhead is not large but the fishing is usually good with the fish holding at certain spots in the river.

Timing for the Pallant starts in December with a small run and continues through April with a few fresh fish in May. I find February the best month with March the next best.

The river is made up of canyon water and a few open gravel runs. To fish the river there are three or four walks. Starting at the downstream end, there is an old road stub about 1 kilometre from tidewater with a good trail into the Cabin Pool. Fish this run down to tidewater or upstream a ways, upstream is difficult going. The next pull off is more difficult to find but it is a trail into the canyon 1.3 kilometres from the Hatchery turn off. Walk into and down to the river and fish both right and left of where the trail comes to the bottom of the hill. When the water is nice and light green, the fish will be holding on the left just after the river narrows. Sometimes the fish will be aggressive and come up to your fly, not to the surface, but close.

Just a few hundred yards upstream but on the road, is the trail into a cutbank run that is worth fishing. You can walk up to where a small tributary comes into the Pallant on the West side, or you can walk back to the road and drive to a place on the road where some overburden has been dumped. Walk into the same tributary by going down an old garbage dump to the river. Once at the river the main walk is to fish from the run in front of you upstream to the hatchery by staying on the east side of the river until you reach the log jam just downstream of the hatchery. In regular flow crossing 100 feet up-stream of the log jam is possible with chest waders. Fishing downstream from the tributary to the cutbank is also possible but not as far. The walk from the tributary to the hatchery will take all morning. Remember the hatchery pool immediately downstream of the hatchery, this pool always holds a few fish.

The other place to fish the Pallant is above the hatchery, through a trail behind their fuel storage tanks at the hatchery, over a log jam upstream to some good runs. I will leave the rest of the river for you to discover, there is good water all over the Pallant.

Weather can affect the Pallant, but it seldom is out because of colour. Lake-headed like the Copper, the Pallant tends to modify her peaks. Good fishing is had in high water and most beats are fishable. Remember the Pallant is closer to the West coast than Sandspit, therefore it rains there more and it is hard to tell where the water level is from Sandspit. The river is quite clear normally so in periods of no rain it can be hard to get the fish to take anything. I always use a sparsely dressed fly so I won't scare the fish in these conditions

I have had some wonderful days fishing Pallant Creek for Steelhead but the most memorable was not about fishing at all.

While fishing one afternoon I was witness to a large female goshawk take a hen mallard right in front of the run I was fishing. This predator was located high on the branch of an alder tree when I came along fishing upstream. I didn't notice the three mallards just upstream behind a log from me, but the goshawk did. As I moved to make my next upstream cast the mallards flushed. The goshawk, because she had height, just stooped out of the tree to pick up speed, rolled inverted about three feet from the water and climbed inverted to intercept the hen from below and behind. The mallard was doing its best to climb out between the trees but no use, there was a burst of duck feathers and they both disappeared behind the next bend in the river. I quickly ran upriver but they were nowhere in sight. The fine duck feathers were still wafting to the river's surface. It all happened in an instant but it was a mind etching experience. I had a front row seat to nature's stage, and I loved every second of it!

Remote Rivers :
The idea of fishing the more remote streams of the Queen Charlottes is very appealing. Drawbacks include cost and variable chance of success.
I have explored some streams on Louise and Moresby Island but there are more streams I have always wanted to try.

Louise Island has two streams worth fishing, **Mathers Creek** and **Skedans Creek.** I have fished Mathers a number of times but not Skedans.

Mathers is a very nice boulder and gravel stream about the size of Pallant Creek but much more open. Fishing starts at the old hatchery site, about a kilometre from the beach. Access is available by boat up the stream, with tidal constraints, or by helicopter to the estuary. The pools are obvious from the hatchery upstream, if you're game, it is a number of miles all the way to Mathers Lake. I have never gone that far but I've heard it can be done.

The run timing is March and April with the fish being on the small side. The stream is good for fly fishing with some beautiful tailouts and good clean bottom. This stream makes a good day's fishing. The water can be low and clear if there hasn't been any rain for a while so I would go after some recent rain. My favorite run is just upstream of the hatchery site behind the big rock.

Skedans Creek is reputed to have good Steelhead in the upper reaches but I can't help with any more information. The timing should be the same, March or April. I know the lower part has slow flow, but I'm not sure of the rest.

I have fished, with success, the **Echo Harbour stream**, in South Moresby, the fish were small but this little stream is a jewel. It's a good hike to the first hole at the bottom of the rapids. Fish are in there in March and April, but remember these are small systems with probably very few Steelhead, so let's leave the dinner plate fish to a system that can stand the pressure.

Salmon River just north of Echo Harbour on Moresby Island holds Steelhead in the Spring like Echo Harbour and is worth checking out if Echo Harbour is on your itinerary. Both of these streams have access from Moresby camp by boat (it's a two hour ride one way in a fast skiff) or again by helicopter to the estuaries at low tide, it may also be practical to charter a float plane for the same purpose.

Before I suggest some more streams to fish, I want to tell you a short story about where to find Steelhead. A few years back when I had a float camp in South Moresby for sports fishing in the summer for coho. We were tied up in the mouth of a small stream, no bigger than a large ditch, and I remember a few pinks would spawn every other year almost intertidally. I had an idea that since we were there all the time maybe we should do a small enhancement project and increase the coho that we didn't think spawned in this ditch. Before getting too hot on the idea I invited Gary Taconia, Salmonid Enhancement Project community involvement officer to do some parr counts to determine the existing stock before we started to help out nature. The results shocked me. There were already so many coho parr in this ditch, putting more in would probably reduce the output, and amazingly, there were also Steelhead in good numbers. So much for wondering where Steelhead live on the Charlottes. If they had colonized this ditch, they are in every water course that flows to the sea. From that day on I have taken the approach that every stream on the Charlottes has Steelhead living in it, with just timing and holding spots left to figure out.

Here are some of the streams or rivers that I think will have Steelhead in the Spring, but need further exploring.

The **Jalun River** on northwest Graham Island. This system is lake headed, fairly long with nice pools I am told.

The Creek at the head of **Crescent Inlet**, South Moresby.

Tasu Creek for the reputed summer runs.

Davidson Creek and **Naden River** in Naden Harbour. We know there are fish there with spring timing, but it is hard to get to with much more exploring to do.

Ain River in Masset Inlet I've fished for trout, but not steelhead. I've hear stories of steelhead in this system and it sure looked good when I was trout fishing.

Close-up of the two most important parts of a Spring salmon (Chinook) : the eye and the teeth.

Photo: Mike Meegan

A steelhead fisherman working a productive Queen Charlotte Island River.

Photo: Mike Meegan

My life long dream! A float camp in Matheson Inlet, South Moresby Island, Queen Charlotte Islands on a calm, foggy morning. Photo :Jon Murray

Matheson Inlet, South Moresby Island, Queen Charlotte Islands on a beautiful, calm sunset from the deck of the float camp. Photo :Jon Murray

Author helicopter fishing a Queen Charlotte Island estuary
for coho with Pierre Forand, my longtime fishing pilot.
Photo: Mike Meegan

A beautiful wild trumpeter swan flies past while quietly fishing for trout.
Photo: Mike Meegan

Sunrise on Skidegate Lake!
Photo: Mike Meegan

Left & Below Fly fishing the Queen Charlotte Islands many alder treed estuaries.

Photo : Mike Meegan

Photo : Mike Meegan

A beautiful Langara Island Spring (Chinook) salmon Tyee size
Photo :Mike Meegan

A typical East-coast Moresby Island Inlet with skiff at anchor.
Photo :Bob Long

Left:
Working the edge
of Skidegate Lake
for lake cutthroat
trout.

Below:
Author and Francois
Ferland landing a
206 pound halibut
Juan Perez Sound,
South Moresby Island.
Lyell Island in the
background.

Photo :Mike Meegan

Photo :Ellen Hume

Section : Trout

Sea-Run Cutthroat Trout

Life Cycle • Fishing Methods & Rivers
Tlell River • Copper River • Yakoun River
Naden Harbour • Other Streams

Life Cycle:

Sea-run cutthroat come to life in the small streams that are home for salmon and steelhead. The cutthroat is probably the regular prey for Coho and steelhead when they are in their fingerling and parr stage. Cutthroats I have seen in streams are much smaller than coho or steelhead.

These little guys assume the lesser water in the pools and riffles that are home for the bigger steelhead and coho, but they grow quickly and find a niche for themselves in many streams on the Charlottes. According to all that I read, the sea-run cutt spends two years in his natal stream before migrating to sea at about 7 to 8 inches. Although no one knows for sure where these small salmonids go once they reach the sea, most everyone thinks they spend some time in the estuaries foraging on the many crustaceans, and sculpins in the shallows. Spawning can take place more than once, but optimally takes place when the cutt has spent a couple of years in the salt water, with the 18 inchers spawning at 6 or 7 years old.

Sea-run Cutthroat are silver bright when they come back from the sea to their natal stream to spawn. It can be difficult to tell them from their resident brothers once the sea-run has spent some time in fresh water. The silver blends to the resident dull greeny brown and their red slash under the jaw will darken. When a sea-run is ocean fresh he will have a very light coloured throat slash even orange in colour.

Most of this can be proven somewhat by the catch experience from the many sea-run cutthroat streams on the Charlottes. Keep in mind that much research is needed to have a better understanding of the Queen Charlotte Island sea-run cutthroat.

I will discuss the most common sea-run cutthroat fisheries in the Charlottes and then suggest some fishing methods.

Fishing Methods & Rivers :

The **Tlell River** is the stream targeted by the sports fisherman for sea-runs in the month of May. The Tlell fish can be caught along the beach seaward from the river on low water, or falling and rising tides, or more traditionally in the downstream portion from the Tlell River bridge at low water. The Wiggins Road access to the river has also provided excellent cutt fishing. I like to fish these strong silver fish with a fly in the riffles and pools all along Beitush Road. This portion of the Tlell is a joy to fly fish, with lots of backcast and shallow enough to wade effectively. Fly choice seems to matter at times, but the only way to figure the right one is trial and error. I start with the standard "Mickey Finn" and branch into tied down minnow, or "Muddler Minnow".

There are still Sea-runs in the Tlell in June but most are losing their silver sea colours and are migrating up-stream to spawn or go back to sea once the Pink and Chum fingerlings have out-migrated.

The **Yakoun River** has a very healthy run of sea-run Cut-throats, but most are caught as incidentals in the Steelhead fishery. These fish are particularly eager to take the common roe bait used by many of the local steelhead fishermen. Sea-run cutts can be caught anywhere that steelhead are caught on the Yakoun, and there is some excellent estuary fishing for them also. I have not tried this fishing but have heard that these bright fish hold in the estuary and the lower river feeding ravenously on the pink and chum fry migrating out of the river to salt water. Light spinning gear would be a good way to catch these fish in both the Yakoun and Tlell Rivers. Using a small spinner or spoon can be very enticing to a sea-run cutthroat but remember how they love to follow without a strike, so fish all the way to your feet. Most sea-runs on the Charlottes show themselves by surface disturbance and therefore can be sight cast, which makes this fishing very exciting.

The **Copper River** holds a run of Sea-run Cutthroats that are present in the stream in May and June. Again fishing these fish as you would the steelhead will be productive. I have tried to outwit the Copper sea-run in the estuary, but with no luck. They are there but we need a more determined fisherman than I. Rumors of many nice fish being caught in the first pools of the Copper estuary during the Sockeye run in May have been told by reliable sources. The "Muddler Minnow" fly is all that is needed for these fish. Cast the fly upstream and fish under tension across the flow until the fly is directly below you, now retrieve quickly in sharp jerks.

I have had six or seven hits as I jerked the fly right to the end of the rod tip, and still not hooked them. That is not the fish's fault, but it sure is exciting fishing. The "Silver Doctor" fly is also a local favorite for this type of fishing.

That sums up the streams that have easy access by road, but I will discuss the few streams that may be worth the difficult access, if you enjoy sea-run cutthroat fishing.

Streams like the Ain, and Jalun Rivers are reputed to have sea-run cutthroats that run in the spring of the year. I'm sure that is true but I can not personally vouch for this fishing.

The premier Sea-run Cutthroat fishing on the Queen Charlottes is in **Naden Harbour.** This makes a lot of good sense to me. There are many good water holding streams in the Naden Harbour basin. Most importantly Naden Harbour has a very large estuary. Cutthroat can be caught at any time of the year out of a small boat along the edge of tide and beach. The perfect cutthroat environment is this biological soup of an estuary.

Fishing for these fish can be effective from half tide falling along the maze of outflow channels from Davidson Creek , Lignite Creek and Naden River.

An old friend that spent many years as a logging camp cook in Naden Harbour and an avid fly fisherman, told me that the fishing for these cutthroat is productive any time of the year somewhere in the estuary, it is just a matter of searching them out. Cast to the obstructions that are noted at low tide because the sea-run cutthroat love to hold next to some underwater feature. Although Naden Harbour is difficult to get to the cutthroat fishing is worth the trip. Peregrine Lodge, a sports fishing camp, is now operating from an old logging camp in Naden Harbour. The camp will be mostly after Spring salmon, but the possibility of fishing these cutthroat is real.

Other Streams :

The two other streams worthy of mention are Mathers Creek on Louise Island in April/May and Skedans Creek, again sometime in the early spring. I have fished both but without success, although I've heard of others that were rewarded. I think timing is very important in this regard, and that has much to do with water conditions. Give them a try if you are interested, but remember the tidal concerns if you go there with a small boat.

Over the years my interest in the cutthroat fishing on the Charlottes has increased dramatically. These little fighters are not steelhead on a fly rod, but they require a bit more finesse to catch and will come to the surface to slash at your fly - that's the part I love!

Lake Fishing for Trout

Mosquito Lake • White Swan Lake
Skidegate Lake • Mayer Lake

Lake Fishing for Trout :

Trout fishing in the streams has been covered under the sea-run Cutthroat section because the resident trout are usually fished in lakes, not in the streams.

The species of trout fished on the Charlottes is the coastal cutthroat.

Most lakes on the Charlottes have a healthy population of these trout. The preferred time to fish cutthroat is in the early spring when lake life starts to be aware of the longer daylight hours. Although fishing is good for cutthroat all summer, they become less aggressive during the summer months and you need to fish deeper for them.

A number of lakes on the Charlottes have access by road and boat ramp, with the others needing air transport by float plane. I will discuss the road access lakes first.

Mosquito Lake is located on the Moresby road(see map) signed as such with an improved boat ramp and camping area. Traditionally the Sandspit Rod and Gun Club has held a trout derby for the children of the Charlottes at the end of May and weighed in numerous fish, many over 3 pounds. These are caught many different ways , trolling with worms, casting or trolling a spoon or spinner, and in some cases trolling a fly. Anywhere in the lake can produce the big fish.

I like to fish the outflow of the Upper Pallant Creek on the north shore of the lake in April and May with a small pink fly of my own design. Casting over the edge of the drop off and retrieving slowly in a lifting action can produce great fun. These cutthroat will sometimes follow the fly right to your feet without striking, and then the same fish will hit the fly as soon as it lands on the water 20 second later with the next cast. This is the spot to take the children to have a good fishing experience. At the western end of the lake is another inflow stream with a beautiful estuary perfect for having a picnic on a sunny day, in addition to some good fishing again just off the drop off. Slowly trolling the edge of the lake with a "Muddler Minnow" or casting a lure towards the shore also produces fish.

Mosquito Lake is an excellent family lake for fishing and camping with all the improvements you can ask for.

On the Moresby Road before you reach Mosquito Lake (3.5 kilometres from the Moresby road turn-off) is a swamp called **White Swan Lake** (marked by a sign). It's difficult to walk to the edge of this so-called lake because of the floating organic soil and grasses that surround the lake. No one should attempt this walk with children or in anything but good shape. It is dangerous and easy to slip through the floating soil and be in a situation much like falling through the ice on a frozen lake.

If you are game there are some very nice large spawning cutthroats in this lake. I have taken these fish with an imitation of a caddis pupa, fished on the bottom with a little movement once in a while or a dry fly of many descriptions. These fish feed ravenously during February and March with the fishing still good in April. For the serious Cutthroat fisherman this lake is a must. I once caught a 22 inch cutthroat in this lake, a beautiful fish, all in its spawning colours. I did not kill this female because these fish can not stand heavy fishing pressure, so please be sensible and minimize the kill. As table fare these swamp cutts rate very low anyway.

Skidegate Lake is the head water for the Copper River and therefore is home to many of the same trout found in the river. The lake is fished for Cutthroat trout that at times look like sea-run cutthroat, but are probably just silver coloured lake residents. Skidegate Lake is fished with a boat. Trolling from a boat will be productive, sometimes fishing the outflow and inflow at the east and west ends of the lake. Casting from shore or the old trestle half way along the lake is the most popular practice. There is an improved boat ramp on Skidegate Lake on the southeast end of the lake opposite the rock pit. It is a steep ramp so a four wheel drive is a good idea. I have fished this lake and enjoyed it considerably, catching many 17 to 19 inch Cutthrout trout along the lily pads at the west end of the lake. Great lake!

Mayer Lake is the only other easily accessible lake on the Charlottes for fishing. I have fished this lake with variable success. Trolling a willow leaf or casting a fly at the outflow is the best advice I can give. Mayer is fished more than other lakes because it is on the main highway and therefore the fishing can be slow. On a calm day Mayer makes for great fishing from a canoe.

Fly-in Trout Lakes

Mathers Lake ○ Skundale Lake
Ian Lake ○ Ain Lake & River

The Queen Charlotte Islands do not have many lakes, but a few are good fishing targets. In this section all the lakes require a float plane or a long hike to obtain access.

This type of fishing requires more organization and a bigger bank account. Arrangements must be made for a drop off and pick-up by float plane and because of costs, usually involves more than two fishermen in a party. I have gone on many of these expeditions and always love the flight in and the adventure of arriving at a lake that you have to yourself. Most of the lakes I will discuss require some type of water transport once you are there. A rubber boat, canoe, or in some cases boats that others have left at the lake for such use are necessary. If you have a fishing partner with a float plane then you can use it to fish off also. Be prepared to stay an extra day or two in case the weather gets bad and your pick-up has to be delayed. Three days of unfit flying weather is about maximum for the Queen Charlottes.

Mathers Lake is relatively close to Sandspit or Queen Charlotte City and therefore is not that expensive to fly to. Mathers Lake is located on Louise Island and is the headwater lake for Mathers Creek. I've flown into Mathers Lake with Marvin Boyd of South Moresby Air Charters a number of times and we have caught cutthroats easily from the aircraft floats. It is difficult to cast a fly line from a float plane, but spin casting works well. The hungry cutthroat will attack anything that shines close to their holding areas. Some of these fish go to15 to 16 inches long. The time of the year for this fishing is traditionally April and May but I'm sure the fishing is good all year round.

The series of lakes on Graham Island that are worth the trip are **Ian Lake, Skundale Lake, Ain River** and **Ain Lake**. These water bodies all empty into the western shore of Masset Inlet. I've flown into Ian Lake and fished Skundale Lake and particularly the short stream between the two lakes, through Skundale Lake and down the Ain River. At the time the water was low so we could not get past some rapids and into Ain Lake. The fishing was good all along this watercourse, particularly at the first rapids in the Ain River. This was a great expedition with five of us going in to catch the big ones. The fish were not that big but they were fun to catch and would greedily take a fly or spinner. Cutthroats in this system are very dark, almost black, the same colour as the water. We fished these lakes and river in March, but the fishing may have been better later when the water is higher. Ian Lake has produced a 6 pound cutthroat according to legend.

The experience from Vancouver Island tells us that there are only a few of these giant trout in each lake and once they have been killed the conditions to replicate these fish never return.

Yakoun Lake (also on Graham Island) is accessible by trail off MacMillan Bloedel's logging road. Check with the employees of MacMillan Bloedel before hiking into Yakoun Lake because the access road may change as logging proceeds.

Access is also by float plane, the closest place being Queen Charlotte City. This is a big lake so you should fly-in a water craft of some type for fishing and transportation.

Stories have huge trout jumping out of the lake at anything like trout food. There are trout there alright, but that many ?

Section : **Halibut**

Life Cycle • Catch Methods • Tackle Size
Location, Tide & Depth • Specific Spots

Life Cycle :

The Pacific Halibut is a new comer to the sportfishing scene, but I believe that this big game fish will become a big target for most north coast sports fishermen. To those of us lucky enough to be born on the north coast, the Halibut has always been a great treat to catch. I caught my first at eleven years old off the side of the gillnetter "Silver Token". She was about 100 pounds and caught on a hand line. Robert Johnston had to shoot this fish before bringing it aboard. I have never forgotten that episode and it may have hooked me on fishing for the rest of my life.

The Pacific Halibut spawn in the ocean, with the females releasing huge numbers of eggs into the pelagic stream. Large females, 200 pounds, or so can produce over a million eggs. These small eggs slowly turn into fish in their larval stage. At this junction the Halibut is still less than an inch long. Females grow to sexual maturity in 12 years and are about 50 pounds. The really large Halibut, over 200 pounds are upwards of 30 years old and always females. Male Halibut tend to be around 50 pounds when caught sports fishing, and they may be as old as the females.

The Halibut is a ground fish that lives on the ocean bottom, but can also be caught in midwater. Halibut prey on squid, crab, shrimp, herring and other prey of opportunity as they sit on the bottom. Halibut migrate from the Bering Sea and Alaska into the Charlotte waters, although some think there are resident halibut all year round. Research confirms that there are many areas where halibut rear as juveniles surrounding the Queen Charlotte Islands. Traditionally the Halibut fishery has started in early spring, March or April, and continue throughout the year. The commercial fishery for this prized species has improved in the last ten years and the sports fisherman that wants to get the giants needs to be on the grounds before the first commercial opening, usually in May.

Catch Methods :

Halibut have traditionally been caught with a handline and a Norwegian jig, the banana shaped silver lure 6 to 10 inches long, terminated with a large triple hook. This lure works well when it is raised and dropped just off the bottom. Variations of this theme include the addition of some bait on the hooks, squid or herring. Mooching a herring just off the bottom will also be effective, especially in a tidal current. A new method is to use a down rigger with a spinning herring and bounce the down rigger's cannon ball along the bottom. Obviously you need to know the bottom you are going to use this method on. This method has bagged some very good sized halibut, a 250 pounder by Brian Eccles of Queen Charlotte City in 1988.

Halibut are caught on standard salmon gear on the Sandspit spit in June and you can catch fish whenever the halibut are feeding in the midwater. Many halibut are caught incidentally when salmon are the target.

Tackle size:

Obviously ten pound test line is under weight for the possibility of a 200 pound halibut, but many halibut are caught with 20 pound test. If you are using a handline, I suggest over 100 pound test, more to protect your hands than anything else. If you are into a big one you will be glad for the large line. I use 40 pound test on my heavy 8 foot, one piece tuna rod, but I am fishing for the 200 plus pound fish. Heavy salmon gear is safe if you hook an average sized halibut, just play them carefully.

There are some precautions when fishing large halibut. Do not bring a large fish into a small boat until it is very dead. A better idea is to tie a rope through the mouth and gills and leave it overboard tied to the boat. Halibut are so strong and difficult to kill that they can destroy a small boat with their characteristic flapping. Most experienced halibut fishermen shoot halibut in the head with a .22 calibre gun (or larger calibre), before boating. I also use a very large shark hook tied to a float that I hook the halibut with the first time I bring it to the surface. This way if the fishing line breaks or the original hook comes out the halibut is still hooked to the float which she will tow around until tired. I have used this safety method on large halibut a number of times with good success.

Catching halibut requires that the fishermen be at a particular location at a particular tide. Most halibut are caught at the low slack and high slack tidal periods. I fish 40 minutes before and after low water slack tide and before and after high water slack tide. The period coming up to low water slack seems to be very effective in addition to the actual slack tide itself.

Locating halibut requires that you decide on the location before the tide and stay with it through the tide cycle. I have jigged for an hour with no action only to have two halibut within 10 minutes of each other right on the tidal slack. The tidal rules may not be that applicable if you choose to use the down rigger troll method. I think the dragging cannon ball may entice a strike from the halibut lying in wait for a meal to happen by.

Knowing the right fishing depth is also important to catch halibut. They can be caught in very shallow water at times, for example, halibut have been caught in Skedans Bay in only 15 feet of water. Very large depths may also hold halibut, but I have always been too lazy to haul my line in and out for any real depth. Using charts are the best way to determine the most likely halibut spots. Look for underwater shoals to 8-10 fathoms in depth, drop-offs from 6 to 18-20 fathoms, or flats at about 12 fathoms.

The composition of the bottom is also important, with gravel and sand being the most productive for halibut. Sometimes charts will give this information, but experience on the grounds will tell you the most. Irregular bottom will hold mostly ling cod and other ground fish, and it will hang-up your fishing gear also.

There are some traditional hot spots for halibut fishing and I will suggest a few here, in addition to the areas outlined on the charts in the body of this book. These areas are not in any way exhaustive, only a start to your halibut fishing.

In May, the areas surrounding the Skidegate ferry landing have been a good bet over the years. The west coast through Skidegate Narrows will always be productive in the Spring, try Marble Island and any likely looking areas on the chart. The reason that these areas are not fished heavily is because the weather makes getting out to the west coast difficult most days.

The Sandspit Spit is good halibut fishing in June for midwater fish. The area east of Miller Creek to the red can-buoy is the traditional halibut spot (even called Halibut Bight) for April with many fish taken every year. The head of Cumshewa Inlet around the red can-buoy, in front of Cumshewa Island, in front of Skedans Point and the shoals between Low Island and Skedans Islands all produce good halibut every year. Once you finish scouting these spots, there are many more that I haven't mentioned.

Red Snapper, Ling Cod, and other ground fish can be caught almost anywhere in Queen Charlotte Islands waters. Ling Cod need a more irregular bottom than halibut and Red Snapper are deeper than halibut. I have noted a couple of Ling Cod spots on the charts in case you want something different to eat.

The Queen Charlotte Islands have been and will continue to be a very good area for halibut fishing, with the possibility of a sports caught fish topping the 300 pound mark. As more and more fishermen become excited about catching the big halibut on light sports gear more areas and fishing methods will be discovered. Maybe in 15 years the number one sportsman's prize will be the Halibut instead of the Spring salmon!

Section : General Information
Launch Ramps • Maps of Steelhead Rivers
• Charts of Ocean Fishing Areas

Launch Ramps :

For quick reference I will list the available boat launching areas. Because the Queen Charlotte Islands are unorganized area there are no public boat ramps as known on the mainland. Many are used for other purposes (amphibian aircraft, for example) that may not be apparent at the time you launch your boat. So pay attention to parking your vehicle out of the way and in the parking lots if available.

Sandspit area :

1. Copper Bay: ramp located as you first come to the Bay, rough at low tide because after half tide the launch area is very flat. Bad in any Southeast wind. Try to launch and come in on high tide. Parking is along the road and is crowded at Derby time in October.

2. Sandspit Dock: this ramp is improved and is a good any tide launch. Westerly wind makes it rough to launch. Park in the designated lot at the top of the ramp.

3. Alliford Bay B.C.Ferries ramp: Commonly used as a boat ramp, this area is designed for ferry use so keep that in mind, and use common sense. There is a parking lot at the top of the ramp please use it.

106

5. South Bay: There are two unimproved gravel ramps 1 1/2 kilometres east and west of the South Bay log dump.

Queen Charlotte Area:

1. Skidegate Ferry Landing Ramp: Again this is a ferry ramp so the same goes for launching as Alliford Bay. Parking is not as well defined but the ferry parking lot is not acceptable, so everyone usually parks on the road.

2. Airplane Ramp: This is half way to Queen Charlotte City from the Ferry and is used almost every day by amphibious aircraft so again use extreme caution and common sense. Parking is a problem here so park as far away from the ramp as you can.

Port Clements Area:

1. Port Clements Dock: Launch at the dock on the east side, or at the dry land sort with permission.

2. Yakoun River Estuary: There is a high water launch off a stub road at the end of the pavement going towards Juskatla.

3. Juskatla Ramp: There is launching grades at the Juskatla camp, but you must obtain permission from MacMillan Bloedel before proceeding.

Tlell Area:

1. There are no real recognized launch areas here but most people launch in front of Wiggins road. Any wind makes this difficult to say the least. Others launch in the river off of Beitush road at high tide but again this has its problems. I recommend that you launch in Queen Charlotte City and run around. Not good but the best there is.

Masset Area:

1. Seaplane ramp on the causeway: There is a good launch ramp at the seaplane base but again access can be a problem. Watch for aircraft on the ramp and park with common sense.

Rennell Sound:

1. There are a number of rough launch sites at Rennell Sound starting at the old logging camp site at the southern end of the road. There is another at the Forest service camp site. These sites are both rough and soft in places, so be careful!

There are a few more rough to very rough and certain tide launch sites but I will leave those to the locals.

Index of Steelhead River Maps

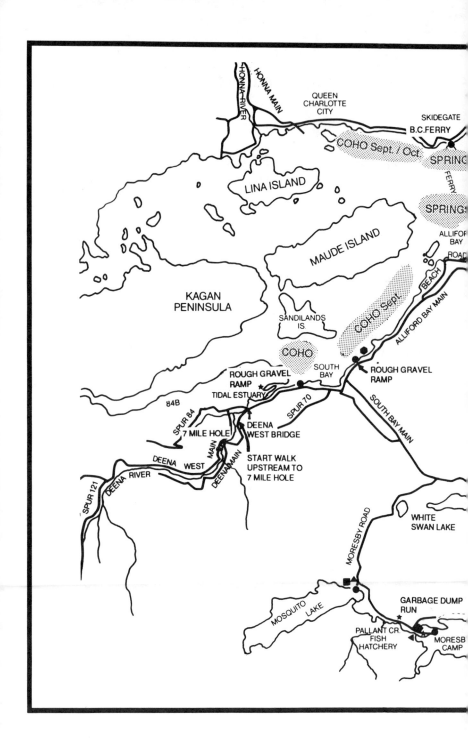

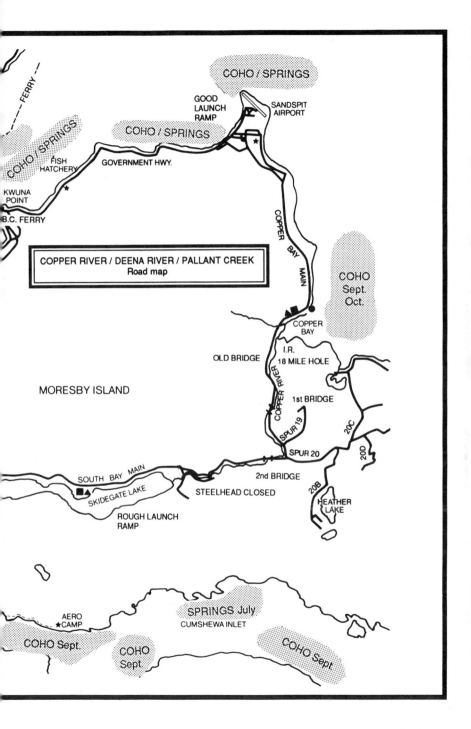

COHO / SPRINGS

GOOD
LAUNCH
RAMP

SANDSPIT
AIRPORT

COHO / SPRINGS

FISH
HATCHERY

GOVERNMENT HWY.

KWUNA
POINT

B.C. FERRY

FERRY

COPPER / SPRINGS

COPPER RIVER / DEENA RIVER / PALLANT CREEK
Road map

COPPER BAY MAIN

COHO
Sept.
Oct.

COPPER
BAY

OLD BRIDGE

I.R.
18 MILE HOLE

MORESBY ISLAND

COPPER RIVER

1st BRIDGE

SPUR 19

20C

20D

SPUR 20

2nd BRIDGE

20B

SOUTH BAY MAIN

SKIDEGATE LAKE

STEELHEAD CLOSED

HEATHER
LAKE

ROUGH LAUNCH
RAMP

AERO
★CAMP

SPRINGS July
CUMSHEWA INLET

COHO Sept.

COHO
Sept

COHO Sept

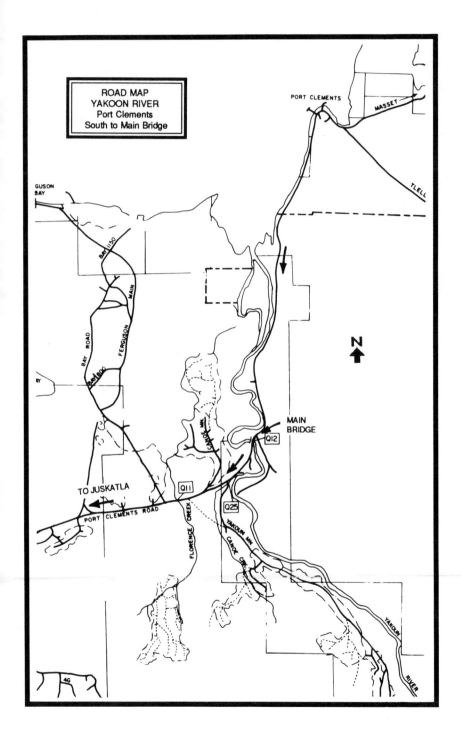

ROAD MAP
YAKOON RIVER
Port Clements
South to Main Bridge

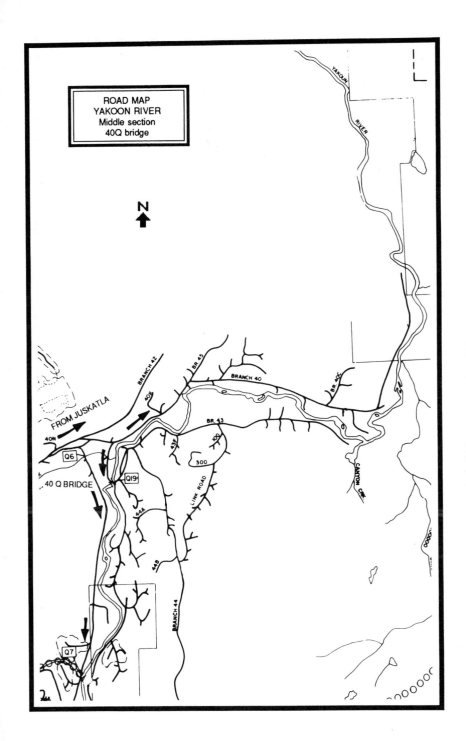

ROAD MAP
YAKOON RIVER
Middle section
40Q bridge

N

113

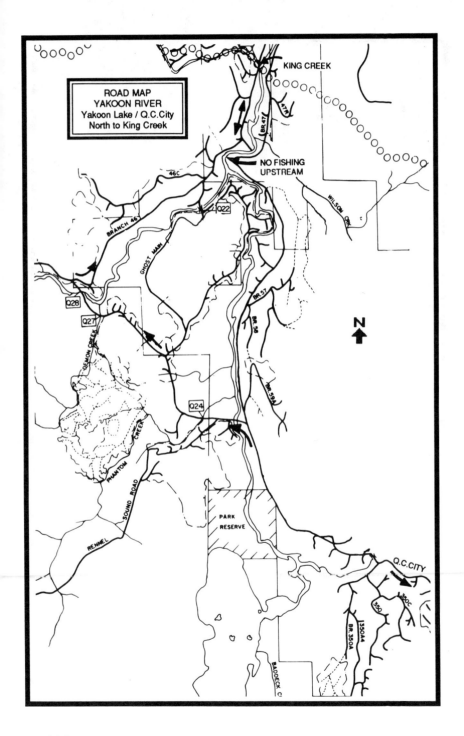

ROAD MAP
YAKOON RIVER
Yakoon Lake / Q.C.City
North to King Creek

KING CREEK

NO FISHING
UPSTREAM

N

114

Index of Fishing Charts

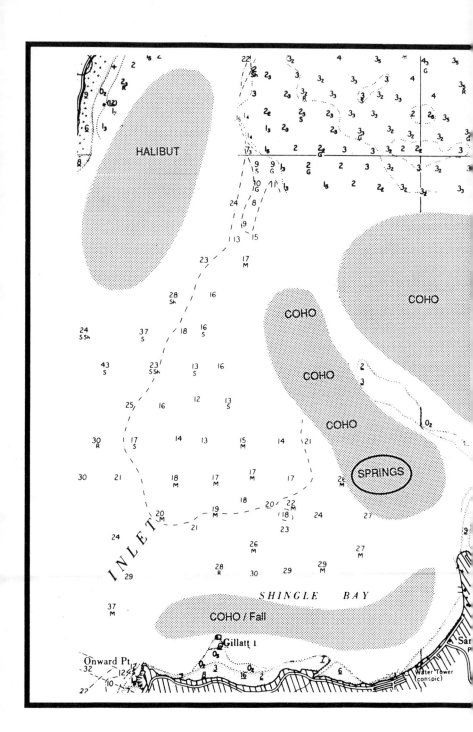

HALIBUT

COHO

COHO

COHO

COHO

SPRINGS

I N L E T

SHINGLE   BAY

COHO / Fall

Gillatt I

Onward Pt

Water Tower
(conspic)

116

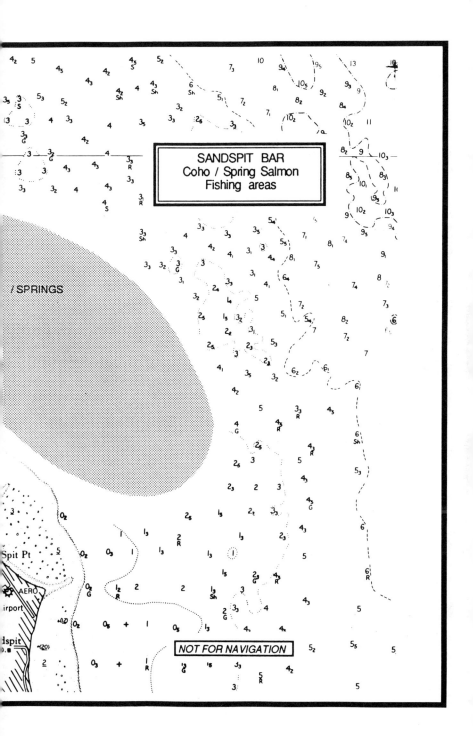

SANDSPIT BAR
Coho / Spring Salmon
Fishing areas

/ SPRINGS

Spit Pt

AERO

irport

dspit

NOT FOR NAVIGATION

117

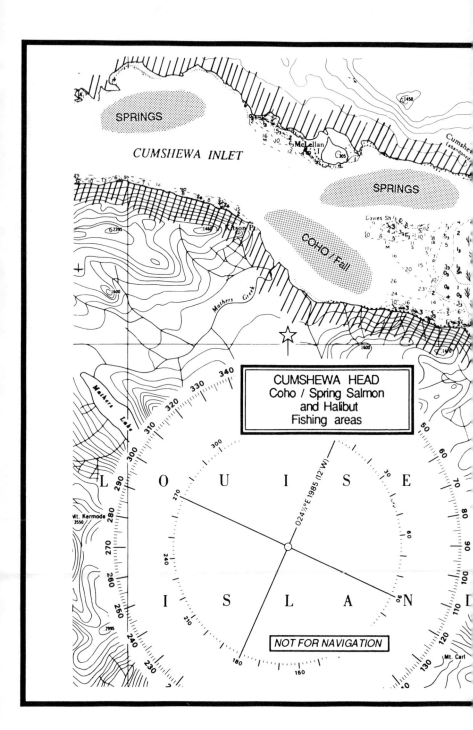

CUMSHEWA INLET

CUMSHEWA HEAD
Coho / Spring Salmon
and Halibut
Fishing areas

SPRINGS

SPRINGS

COHO / Fall

NOT FOR NAVIGATION

L O U I S E

I S L A N D

118

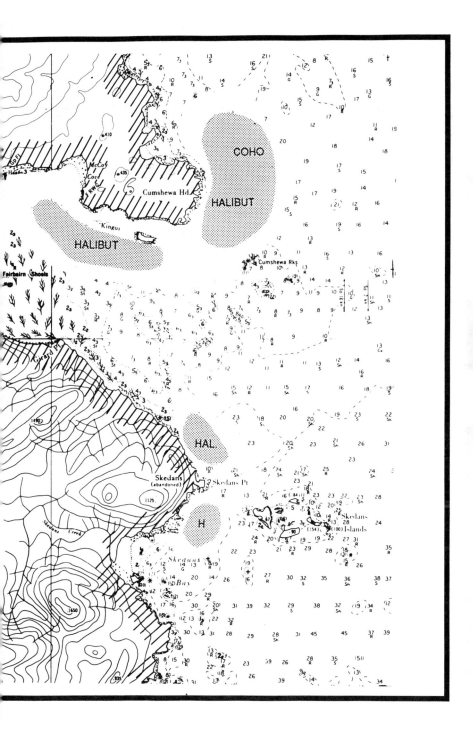

119

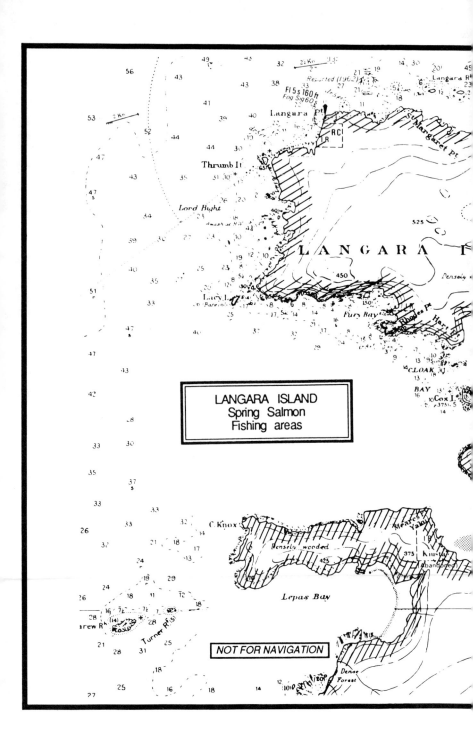

LANGARA ISLAND
Spring Salmon
Fishing areas

NOT FOR NAVIGATION

120

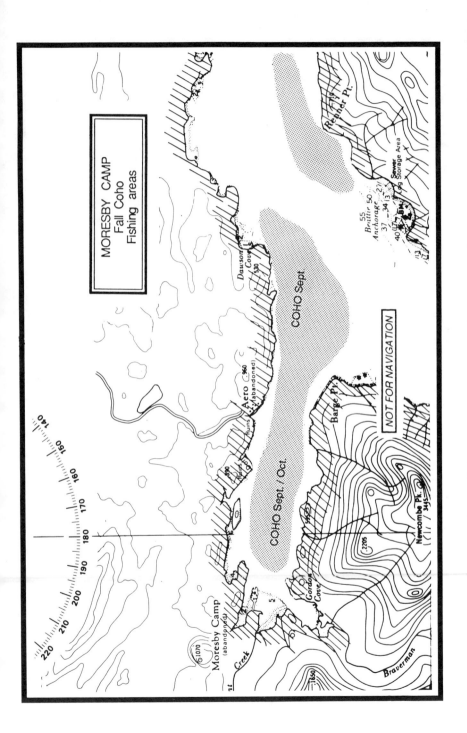

MORESBY CAMP
Fall Coho
Fishing areas

NOT FOR NAVIGATION

COHO Sept

COHO Sept./Oct.

Reither Pt.

Brittle 50
Anchorage
55
37 34 13
40

Sewer
Log Storage Area

Dawson
Cove
530

Aero 960
(abandoned)

Ruins

Ruins 960

Barge Pt.

Newcombe Pt. 3445

2205
1405

Gordon
Cove

5

6

Braverman

Moresby Camp
(abandoned)

Creek

1070

1650

140
150
160
170
180
190
200
210
220

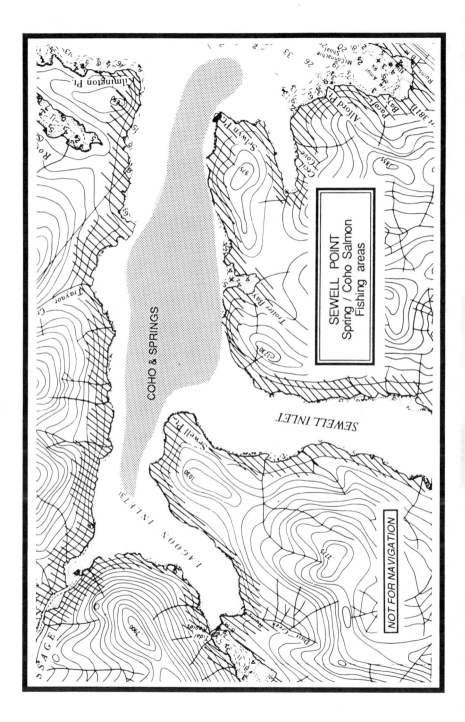

SEWELL POINT
Spring / Coho Salmon
Fishing areas

NOT FOR NAVIGATION

123

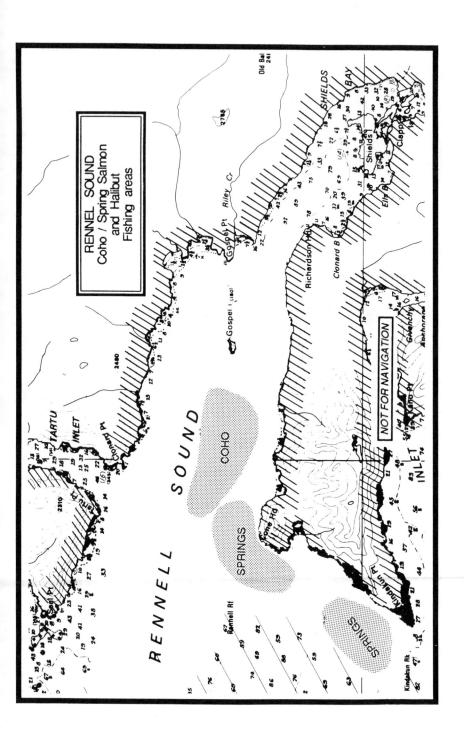

RENNEL SOUND
Coho / Spring Salmon
and Halibut
Fishing areas

NOT FOR NAVIGATION

RENNELL SOUND

COHO

SPRINGS

SPRINGS

TARTU INLET

SHIELDS BAY

124

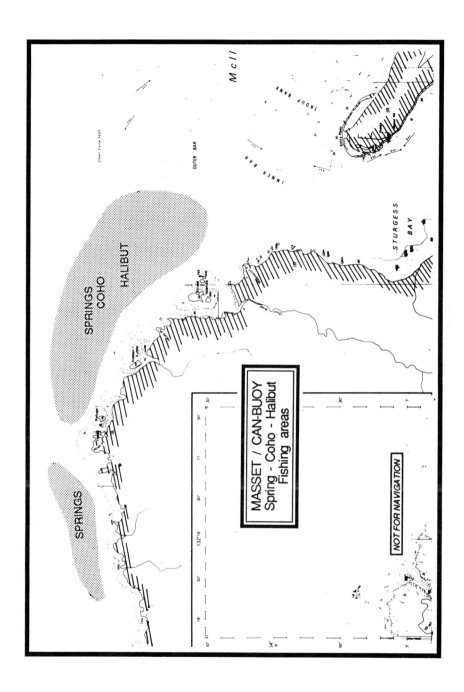

MASSET / CAN-BUOY
Spring - Coho - Halibut
Fishing areas

NOT FOR NAVIGATION

125

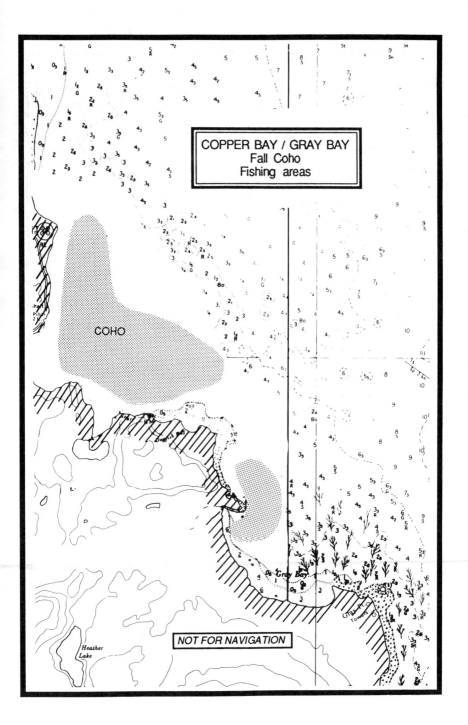

COPPER BAY / GRAY BAY
Fall Coho
Fishing areas

COHO

NOT FOR NAVIGATION

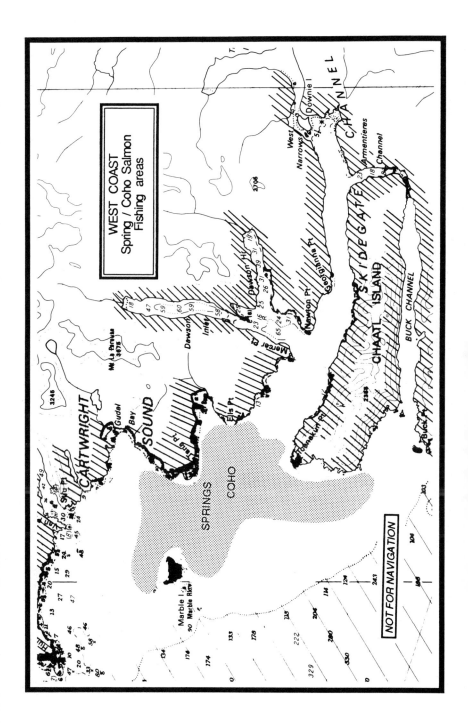

WEST COAST
Spring / Coho Salmon
Fishing areas

NOT FOR NAVIGATION

NOTES